Creativity and Cr Thinking

D1649648

WINCHESTER

What do we mean by creativity? What is the link between creativity and critical thinking? How can creativity and critical thinking be incorporated into classroom practice and what are the benefits for students?

Creativity and critical thinking are central to effective teaching and learning and have a significant impact on students' attainment, engagement, attendance and behaviour. This book draws on recent research and policy to provide teachers with a clear framework for understanding creativity and critical thinking and practically demonstrates how they can be incorporated into classroom practice.

Bringing together an expert team of contributors with a wide range of experience of bringing creative approaches into the classroom, the book includes:

- an analysis of the issues associated with creativity and critical thinking;
- clear guidance on how schools can develop dynamic thinking and creative learning strategies and use them with all learners;
- advice on using external agencies to bring the creative perspective into schools;
- case studies alongside examples of current activities and practice in schools;
- links to resources and organisations who can offer support.

Providing clear guidance on the underpinning theory and policy and drawing upon current initiatives in schools, this book is essential reading for trainee and practising teachers that want to provide the best possible learning experience for their students.

Steve Padget is an independent Education Consultant and Quality Assurance Tutor at Merseyside and Cheshire Graduate Teacher Programme. He was previously Lecturer in PGCE Secondary English at Liverpool Hope University.

Teaching contemporary themes in secondary education series

The secondary national curriculum encourages teachers to develop more creative and flexible teaching around interrelated themes, which will help young people to make sense of some of the key ideas and challenges in today's world.

This series explores the key themes of global learning and sustainable development, creativity and critical thinking, technology and the media, identity and cultural diversity, and enterprise.

Each theme represents a key topic considered to be of particular relevance to young people growing up in the twenty-first century. These themes are not intended to be curriculum subjects, but rather over-arching themes that bring a greater sense of relevance and interconnectedness to the way in which young people learn.

These books aim to explore such themes in some depth, investigating how they link to different areas of the curriculum (including different education agendas) while giving an overview of policy changes and implications for practice. They provide ideas on how to incorporate these themes through a whole-school approach, using practical case studies of a range of activities and approaches, with detailed information on how this was organised and implemented and the outcomes and learning achieved.

About the editors

Helen Gadsby is the course leader for the PGCE secondary geography course at Liverpool Hope University. She also teaches on the BAQTS and PGCE primary courses. She has 16 years' teaching experience in secondary schools, where she held positions of Head of Geography and Head of Year. Helen's research interests include education for sustainable development and global learning. She has presented workshops and papers around these topics at a number of national and international conferences.

Andrea Bullivant works for Liverpool World Centre, an organisation that works with schools, communities and organisations to raise awareness about issues of global interdependence and global justice. As part of this role she has worked closely with the Education Faculty at Liverpool Hope University to embed global learning within LHU's teacher training and education courses. More recently this work has involved developing CPD training for teachers on global learning themes and supporting the work of LHU's Centre for International and Development Education (CfIDE).

Creativity and Critical Thinking

Edited by Steve Padget

Routledge
Taylor & Francis Group

LONDON AND NEW YORK

First published 2013
by Routledge
2 Park Square, Milton Park, Abingdon, Oxon OX14 4RN

Simultaneously published in the USA and Canada
by Routledge
711 Third Avenue, New York, NY 10017

Routledge is an imprint of the Taylor & Francis Group, an informa business

© 2013 Steve Padget

British Library Cataloguing in Publication Data
A catalogue record for this book is available from the British Library

Library of Congress Cataloging in Publication Data
Creativity and critical thinking / Edited by Steve Padget.
   p.cm.
   Includes bibliographical references.
   1. Creative ability. 2. Critical thinking. I. Padget, Steve, editor of
compilation.
   F408.C75445 2012   2012017739
   370.11'8–dc23

ISBN: 978–0–415–69282–3 (hbk)
ISBN: 978–0–415–69283–0 (pbk)
ISBN: 978–0–203–08302–4 (ebk)

Typeset in Bembo and Helvetica Neue
by Bookcraft Ltd, Stroud, Gloucestershire

MIX
Paper from
responsible sources
FSC
www.fsc.org   FSC® C004839

Printed and bound in Great Britain by
TJ International Ltd, Padstow, Cornwall

For Julie

Contents

Notes on Contributors

Brin Best is an education consultant and award-winning author, with a special interest in creativity. He is the co-author of the *Creativity for Learning* series of books for Continuum International Publishing. Brin is also the author of ten other books for classroom teachers and school managers, and was co-originator of the critically acclaimed *Teachers' Pocketbooks*. Prior to setting up his consultancy company, Brin worked in schools and local education authorities as a teacher, head of department and Gifted and Talented coordinator. Brin works tirelessly to help create a brighter future for young people in our schools and is convinced of the value of creativity and critical thinking in helping people to reach their potential. You can learn more about his work at www.brinbest.com.

Kirsty Coomber currently works at St Wilfrid's Academy in the northwest. Her role as Director of the Training School gives her frequent opportunities to work with ITTs, NQTs and RQTs at her own school and within the borough. She leads on whole-school learning and teaching, predominantly focusing on strategies to ensure learners are actively engaged in the learning process. Kirsty's background lies within the expressive arts; however, she is currently looking at the implementation of personal learning thinking skills within the Year 7 curriculum at the Academy.

Rebecca Fearon is Head of Participation at the Bluecoat, an arts centre in the heart of Liverpool. In this role Rebecca is responsible for strategic development and day-to-day management of the organisation's participation programme, involving work with schools, communities and families. Rebecca graduated in 1996 from the University of Surrey with a BMus (first class) and worked for the London Festival Orchestra as Education and Outreach Officer before taking up the post as Director of the R.C. Sherriff Rosebriars Trust, an arts development trust in Surrey. Rebecca relocated to Liverpool in 2004 and was excited to be part of Liverpool's year as European

Capital of Culture when the Bluecoat reopened in 2008 after a three-year capital development.

Carmel Anne Hodson is in her sixth year of teaching at English Martyrs RC Primary School and is responsible for ICT and MFL, but also likes to get involved with mentoring children and trainee teachers. She enjoys reading and attempting to be artistic and is still trying to become a decent cook. Carmel Anne loves working with children, enjoying how every day they can make you laugh or take you by surprise, and never stops learning from the children she is privileged to work with.

Andrea McLoughlin is in her tenth year of teaching at English Martyrs RC Primary School. She is responsible for Music, Gifted and Talented pupils and mentoring of trainee teachers. Learning something new every day about teaching is still the reason she loves her job. Outside school time, she enjoys riding her pedal bike – a new skill only just learnt – being creative and testing out recipes on unsuspecting guests. Time spent with family and friends is the most precious time of all.

Steve Padget is an independent consultant and writer based in the northwest and specialising in thinking skills and creative learning. He promotes the idea that the teacher's appreciation of the importance of the role of language and its relation to thinking has a profound effect on pupils' learning across the curriculum. Having taught English in inner-city schools for over 30 years, Steve developed a keen interest in the details of the learning process while working on Liverpool's Gifted and Talented programme and at the same time working on Key Stage 3 test development. Steve has for many years been involved in the training of new teachers, recently with Liverpool Hope University and currently with the Merseyside and Cheshire GTP consortium.

Will Thomas is a performance coach, trainer and author with a passion for coaching and creativity in education. An award-winning and best-selling author and co-author of nine books in the fields of coaching, creativity and leadership, he is also an international speaker and authority on organisational coaching approaches in education. He works closely with schools, teachers and young people to research and develop creative thinking skills and solutions-focused approaches to challenges. Will is passionate about making a difference to the lives of young people and believes in equality of access to learning and thinking skills for all learners. You can learn more about his work at http://visionforlearning.co.uk

Preface

The driving force behind this book is my firm belief in the primacy of language in the learning process and how this links with creative learning and teaching and critical thinking. Reading the work of such luminaries as Robin Alexander and Neil Mercer changed the way I looked at the whole of the learning and teaching enterprise. I was made to reassess the theoretical underpinning of my practice and begin to look at learning in a different way. This change in me was reinforced by practical experience in the classroom across a wide range of settings, deliberately using and assessing creative thinking techniques. The comments I frequently got from class teachers often mentioned how much better they felt the group had worked, how much more enthusiasm and engagement had been apparent, and how much better they had learned. This feeling was echoed by the learners themselves and confirmed by my own observations. There is a welter of research material readily available to add true academic weight to my anecdotal evidence, as well as a strong body of opinion that is clearly articulating the necessity for educators to think differently about how learners learn, what they need to know and how that should be taught.

This volume begins and ends with questions that teachers should be asking about creativity and critical thinking in order to broaden their understanding of these two important concepts. In between is a gathering together of ideas and experiences that will provide some answers, some jumping-off points for thoughts and action, maybe further reading and, inevitably, some more questions. The reader will quickly realise that the working concept of creativity encompasses all curricular areas, that it is intimately related to critical thinking and that the understanding of this is both a cultural and a philosophical starting point on which effective pedagogical practice can be built.

Each chapter looks at a different aspect of these concepts and will help the reader to see how the growing understanding of creativity and critical thinking has the potential for transformational impact on classroom practice. The varied nature of the chapters reflects the variety of interpretations of creativity that exist in the context of learning. Although the contributions come from different vantage points of experience, the commonality is that each writer demonstrates that creative learning and teaching is about adopting a particular mindset that values each individual learner's potential and that this stance has a profound effect on the planning, the nature and the effectiveness of learning experiences. It is hoped that the reader, whether reading the book as a whole or dipping into it (it has been designed to work either way), will see the strength of belief held by this group of writers as they delve into their practice and share their experiences.

An introduction to creativity and critical thinking

In Chapter 1 the territory is mapped out and we take a look at some of the research-based and philosophical roots noting the influence that the work of Vygotsky has had on educational thinking, particularly in the last ten years or so. The chapter then considers the factors that need to be taken into account when trying to arrive at working definitions of first creativity, then critical thinking. In doing this we see the components of both, deconstructed and with a view to examining what they tell us about the processes of learning. We see what learning could be like in a creative classroom and discuss the relative merits of immersion and infusion as ways to develop critical thinking in learners. We see the paradigm shift that is needed if the vision of a creativity-driven, learner-centred pedagogy is to be achieved in anything other than small and scattered pockets of excellence. The concept of a 'Thinking School' is introduced and we see what that title tells us about what goes on in such places and how the members of those learning communities articulate their rationale.

Creativity in – creativity out

Chapter 2 is relevant to the work of all teachers but may be particularly useful for those in training or in the early years of their careers. It looks at the importance of recognising the life-changing impact that the decision to train as a teacher will have on an individual; it looks at the need to develop a clear personal philosophy of learning and suggests ways in which this will influence the teacher's relationships with learners and their learning. The critical role of language as the primary cultural tool is discussed in the context of social learning and the implications of this are examined in respect of classroom dynamics, the position and role of the teacher in the classroom jigsaw, and the quality of learning. The reluctance of many teachers and many schools to acknowledge that changes are necessary is commented on, citing the findings from Wolfe and Alexander's research in 2008. That talk is the essence of learning is emphasised and linked directly to creative approaches and the component skills of critical thinking. The chapter concludes by offering generic advice and guidance on how lesson plans can be interrogated when planning for creative learning.

A framework for creativity in schools

In Chapter 3, two prolific writers on the subject of creativity in the classroom begin by looking at what creativity is (and what it is not) from the point of view of the practising teacher. The barriers to creativity that are in the minds of both learners and teachers are examined and ways of overcoming these are detailed as the processes of creativity are encapsulated in the eight-step Creativity Cycle. The chapter concludes by looking at the implications for school leaders wanting to nurture learners' creativity in the working practices of their schools.

Sowing the seeds

If the phrase 'lifelong learner' is to mean anything, we have to understand that the learning journey is a continuum and that there are implications for cross-phase understanding, cooperation and coordination that go far beyond the arrangements that are usually made. Chapter 4 shows how creative learning is often collective, how it is not, strictly speaking, measurable and that it is not subject specific. The sophisticated work that goes on in many primary schools with the benefits that accrue to learners, teachers and the wider community is exemplified here in a detailed examination of two major Creative Partnership-assisted projects.

A question of integration

Teachers new to the profession face a great many obstacles in the early years of their service and pressures to perform that can often have a narrowing effect on the development of their learning and teaching skills repertoire. Chapter 5 describes how the current promotion of M-level studies provided the motivation for two young teachers to explore the use of creative learning techniques. Guided by their mentor in school, valuable experience was gained as the teachers co-planned and co-taught learning episodes that specifically addressed the implications for methodology that creativity and critical thinking bring. In this work the creativity of the teachers is shown not only in the planning of learning, but also in the vision of scale and scope as they move the session away from the confines of both the school building and the school timetable.

New faces in new places

The writer of Chapter 6 shows some of the impact and benefits that accrue to teachers, learners and creative professionals when some of the major recommendations of *All Our Futures* (NACCCE 1999) are implemented. Creative, dynamic and interventional approaches can have influences across the traditional subject boundaries, and can be made to touch the lives of those learners whom schools find hard to reach and we see how the work, experience and influence of creative professionals can enrich the training of teachers. The Ofsted report (2006) assessing the impact of Creative Partnerships comments on the enrichment and integration of the curriculum that takes place when creative projects are undertaken. It is hard to overstate the value of the role of creative hubs, such as the Bluecoat in Liverpool, in providing the links between creative professionals and schools; or the role played by a supportive school management and staff in the delivery of such projects. The multiple benefits that are enjoyed by learners are manifest and enhanced levels of cooperation, self-confidence, team work and enthusiasm are mentioned specifically in the report as being some of these.

Barriers, enablers and practical approaches

In the desire to pull all the threads of the foregoing chapters together, Chapter 7 begins by looking again at the relationship between creativity and critical thinking, at the implications for learning embedded in these concepts, and at how this understanding can have a transformational effect on classroom practice. It continues with an examination of the enablers of creativity that exist and also the barriers to creative learning that are frequently found and have to be overcome. The chapter goes on to discuss the positive and creative dimensions and possibilities that are opened up by a range of influential learning methodologies and the support that these provide for the creative teacher. In reaching the conclusion that creativity and critical thinking are related dynamic concepts, that they are integral to the processes of learning and that a clear understanding of them can be seen as a powerful force for change in teaching, three questions are posed that need to be addressed if that change is to be achieved.

Creativity is a lot to do with personality, how people approach problems and issues, how they use new combinations of ideas to arrive at solutions, and how they are motivated. Creative teachers are intrinsically motivated; they are not content with the status quo and are comfortable with the idea of moving away from it. The chapters in this book demonstrate the importance of being able to see possibilities across a range of environments and to be motivated to achieve objectives that have value, utility and novelty.

References

National Advisory Committee on Creative and Cultural Education (NACCCE) (1999) *All Our Futures: Creativity, culture and education* (The Robinson Report), London: HMSO.

Ofsted (2006) *Creative Partnerships: Initiative and impact.* London: Ofsted.

1

An introduction to creativity and critical thinking

Steve Padget

Key questions

- What is creativity and how does it manifest itself in the classroom?
- What is critical thinking and how does it relate to creativity?
- What implications are there for the design and delivery of learning?

Initial thoughts

Before we begin to look at the definitions of creativity and critical thinking we need to look at three factors that contribute to what could be called the landscape of learning as we see it in the school context; they are the learning environment, the learning curriculum and the content curriculum.

The learning environment is the result of a combination of factors – physical, social, intellectual and cultural. It will be shaped by details brought by the learners: the orientation and stimulation provided by their own histories, their surroundings and the quality and range of social interactions that they enjoy. These together provide the learner with what they know, and what they bring with them, and it is essential that teachers value this and know what happens outside the confines of the school in the world of the learners they work with.

Then there is the learning curriculum; this consists of the active development of those habits of mind, those interests, values and beliefs and the sense of identity that a learner brings with them, often, initially, unformed and lacking in direction. These are the learner's dispositions; they are malleable and changeable, and can be developed and nurtured to form the habits of mind that will fuel the learning journey. In his extended introduction to Freire's *Pedagogy of Freedom* (1998) Stanley Aronowitz argues that the aim of education must be to contribute to the development of the active knower and to do this the learner's dispositional starting point has to be known.

Finally, there is the content curriculum: that body of knowledge, skills, ideas and concepts that are to be taught over a given period – the cognitive tasks of the learning journey. Although, to some, the National Curriculum can be seen as being restrictive and content driven, there are many who have approached the necessary task of delivery in imaginative and creative ways to the benefit of themselves and the learners they work with. Schools that have adopted a creative learning ethos, for example Schools of Creativity and Thinking Schools, are succeeding in delivering the National Curriculum in ways that richly benefit the learners in all aspects of their cognitive, social and dispositional development.

Creative learning and teaching starts with the adoption of a particular view and understanding of the dynamics of the learning process and examines the relationship that exists between teachers and learners in that process. We need, therefore, to examine the positions of creativity and critical thinking in the stimulation and support of what has been called 'deep learning' as the three factors above are brought together. The following points serve two purposes; they open up the discussion about the subject and in so doing they give purpose to the chapter.

- Teachers are being creative when they are using pedagogical approaches that involve both themselves and learners in looking at possibilities, looking for flexibility, taking risks and experimenting. Creativity is being employed when there are unusual and exciting learning opportunities that provide high-quality stimuli combined with the structure to generate enquiring language and provide deep support for the learners' thinking and efforts.

- Learners are being creative when they are fully engaged in making meaning together through stimulating learning tasks of which they feel ownership. They will feel confident enough to make speculations and assertions, and feel empowered to articulate their learning to any of the other people round them.

- Learners are thinking critically when they step back and reflect on what they have achieved in relation to a desired outcome; when they can discuss and evaluate these achievements either individually or collectively against appropriate criteria and be conscious of, and be able to comment on, the quality of the process of which they have been a part.

■   What links each of these ideas is the planned and deliberate use of language stemming from a clear understanding of its importance as an integral part of thinking and learning in a social context.

The teacher's traditional position as didact and fount of knowledge is no longer an acceptable model. This caricature figure pouring knowledge into tousled and leaking heads has given way to an image of the teacher who is in tune with learners, and who will enter into discussion with learners and provide the appropriate interactive learning opportunities and levels of support in the pursuit of those same learners' agreed aims – the 'sage on the stage' has given way to the 'guide on the side' (King 1993), the monologic has given way to the dialogic and the transmission model of teaching has been superseded by a more effective, learner-centred interpretational approach.

The repositioning of the teacher has only come about because of the changes that have taken place in the understanding of the learning process and the theories of learning that have been developed from research, massive in scope and minute in detail. The developmental process that is education continues to have a number of drivers that we are all well aware of; philosophical, cultural, ethical and moral as well as political and economical influences are present in the ways that national education is organised and the ways that learning in the classroom is managed. While it has to be said that not all of these influences are always in harmony, there is evidence in classrooms of the greater understanding of some very important learning and teaching principles that have initiated positive developments in practice for the benefits of learners and teachers alike.

The understanding now, led by such bodies as the Campaign for Learning, is that, rather than accumulating knowledge as such, learners should be guided towards the acquisition of skills and competences that are needed to access, select, process and evaluate information relating to the knowledge they seek and this aim should be pursued as diligently as the teaching of the knowledge itself. These have been identified as Claxton's '4 Rs' or the 'learning dispositions' of Resilience, Resourcefulness, Reflectiveness and Reciprocity (Gornall *et al.* 2005). These are the starting points of self-awareness that are available for use when tackling a cognitive task – and teachers need to have a practical understanding of these dispositions, and of their role in modelling and nurturing the development of these life skills in learners. The phrase 'learning to learn' comes to mind here and the metacognitive implications associated with that. Just as part of the teacher's role is to enable learners to reflect upon their learning and to understand how they have achieved and what they have achieved against the appropriate criteria, they too must make critical reflections on their practice. Those dispositions possessed of the teacher must allow them to be the teacher-learner as well as the learner-teacher, for 'there is no teaching without learning' (Freire 1998: 29).

There are those who still imagine knowledge as a personal possession acquired in private, but increasingly the view is that knowledge is a social entity – something shared – 'the essence of human knowledge is that it *is* shared' (Mercer

2006: 6) and as such is part of the human sociocultural fabric. Willis argues that 'within the sociocultural paradigm, learning is viewed as the process of participating in a community of practice, where expertise is developed in social as well as cognitive ways through use of cultural tools learned by working alongside more expert members' (2009: 1).

This, in a nutshell, is the social constructivist view of learning, rooted in the work of Vygotsky and based on the understanding that learners are active creators of meaning and the principal cultural tool is language. Subscribing to this strongly held and well-supported view demands that we assess what we mean by *learning* (the noun), as well as *learning* (the verb), and be aware of the profound implications for the pedagogies that are adopted in response to that understanding. Learning and teaching arrangements should be used that strive to facilitate meaning making in a social context and the development of the classroom as a community of enquiry where social methodologies are the norm and learners move to an understanding of the power of their own language as creative learning and critical thinking takes place.

Creativity and critical thinking can, in my view, be regarded as two sides of the same coin. Nickerson says that 'it can be argued that to think well requires both creative and critical capabilities, that neither can be effective without the other' (1999: 398). These are not therefore mutually exclusive personal attributes and part of the role of the teacher is to provide the appropriate stimuli and environment that will allow both to develop in concert. The development of these will define the individual in life.

Towards a definition of creativity

While it may be considered impossible to define the process of creativity, the creative outlook of a person and the products of creativity are observable (Feist 1999) and it is in the nature, quality and context of these products – the thoughts, actions and outcomes – that our definition will ultimately lie. The learning process itself, according to Paulo Freire, should be regarded as a creative force.

The concept of the highly creative individual, the person locked away and alone, producing work of aesthetic beauty or scientific magnitude, is a romantic vision and does not help our cause when we are trying to find a realistic, workable, contemporary definition of creativity. Most modern human achievements are the result of team work; groups of individuals – jigsaw puzzles of different and coordinated talents and aptitudes, experiences and enthusiasms – work together with a shared vision to create a feature film, a TV advert, a motorcar, a drug to fight disease, or a curriculum; these are the results of collaborative creativity. 'It would be a mistake … to view creation as a wholly individual act. In many ways creation also involves co-creation' (Carter 2004: 27). To this we should add, therefore, that 'creative thinking involves cognitive processes that occur in a context. These processes involve novelty in one or more of the processes that lead to creative outcomes' (Halpern 2003: 398).

Since the 1950s, and specifically since the work of J.P. Guilford (1950), the idea of creativity as being something that all learners possess in some degree has gathered pace and over the years the definition of what is meant by the term 'creativity' in an educational context has become refined even though, as we search the literature, we see that the term is still subject to multiple definitions. Arthur Cropley (2001) talks of 'general creativity' as being that quality possessed of all people in some measure as a function of an individual's personality and intellect and the relationship they have with the varied components of their cultural environment. He contrasts this with 'assertive creativity' – that which we would associate with the possession of talent and the particular achievements of artists, writers, musicians and architects, for example. This is echoed in Anna Craft's writing when she talks about 'big C creativity' and 'little c creativity' (2003: 117); the point here being that the latter is that day-to-day quality in everyone, learner and teacher alike, that is the germ of learning.

The relationship between creativity and intelligence has been discussed in great detail and researchers have variously seen it as being an integral part of intelligence or as a separate but related entity; it is widely accepted now that creativity is an important element in the mental make-up of everyone. To confuse intelligence with creative talent is a common error and research has shown that there is little correlation between creativity and IQ scores. Yes, creativity is a key human feature but it is important to realise that a learner's creativity will not develop to full potential if the right conditions are not provided for this to take place. The implication therefore is that schools need to understand the importance of explicitly and directly nurturing the creativity of the pupils and the teachers within the institution.

Creativity and critical thinking go hand in hand and help to provide different ways of making sense of a situation; after applying analytical and logical critical thinking to our problem we can move towards the construction of a solution using our creative thinking. This is the place where creativity and critical thinking meet as we then go on to assess whether the solution we have arrived at is the best solution available. We will know this because we will have applied our critical thinking to the results of our creative thoughts. As we edge towards a working definition of creativity that will be meaningful in the context of learning and teaching, it is essential that we focus on the dispositions of both the teacher and the learner and appreciate how these impact on the products of their creative endeavours, knowing that in school these are intimately linked. Carter (2004) echoes the work of Cropley when he says that in the definition of creativity we must look at the idea of novelty. Cropley (1999) talks about 'effective novelty' and how, when novelty can satisfy certain criteria (technical, professional, aesthetic, scholarly), it can lead to creativity. Rather than 'effective', Carter prefers Sternberg's (1999: 3) use of the term 'appropriate' in his definition: 'creativity is an ability to produce work that is *novel* and *appropriate*' (2004: 47; my italics). In his review of a range of eminent definitions of creativity, Mayer (1999) finds that the features of originality and novelty are repeated again and again as being key components of creativity, as are those of usefulness, significance, appropriateness, value and utility. Further, the '*adaptive* criterion is [also] necessary to distinguish truly creative thinking from merely different and/or pathological thinking' (Feist 1999: 274; my italics).

Our working definition of creativity needs to be capable of describing something that can be applied to all areas of learning and include those experiences that take place beyond the school environment, in neighbourhoods, in communities (both real and virtual) and in homes. By doing this we avoid giving the idea that creativity is something belonging only to the school environment and the learning experiences that take place in school.

We need to think of the following as factors to bear in mind when working towards a definition of creativity in the context of learning and teaching:

- **Creativity is part of the school ethos**
  There must be an understanding that, when effective, there is an ethos in the school that values highly and allows for the sustained and long-term development of creative pedagogic skill and experience: 'Creativity is wasted if it simply translates into the occasional burst of light relief' (Claxton *et al.* 2008: 168).

- **Creativity is common to all**
  The assumption must be that the ordinary person can be creative (Craft 2003) and it is our general creativity that allows us to handle the novelty of everyday situations of problem recognition and problem solving, combined with the ability to evaluate possible solutions and reflect on the success of our actions (Halpern 2003).

- **Creativity is social**
  It needs to be appreciated that the landscape of effective creative learning is a social landscape and that we learn better when we learn together. The social setting might be a school classroom, but equally important is the family setting and that of the neighbourhood, community, culture and the wider physical and cyber environment.

- **Creativity is rooted in the use of language**
  The definition must also recognise that language, and specifically the dialogic use of language, is a fundamental component of creative thought and of learning: 'dialogue becomes not just a feature of learning, but one of its most essential tools' (Alexander 2004: 14).

- **Creativity is closely linked with critical thinking**
  Our definition has to be able to recognise that creativity and critical thinking are linked and when we promote and facilitate the one, we necessarily promote the other.

- **Creativity is seen in the learning approaches adopted**
  In the context of school our definition needs to be suggestive of that range of pedagogies that will tap into, harness, exercise and thus strengthen the general creativity that exists in all teachers and learners and do this in a

dynamic way, but the focus should be on the ordinary rather than the extraordinary (Craft 2003).

■ **Creativity is seen differently in different cultures**
There needs to be an understanding that creativity is not culture neutral. There should be recognition of the current trend of many national educational policies around the globe to include explicit references to the value of creativity in an educational context. This has been seen as indicative of the growing power of Western liberal individualism and the cultural value set and view of self that this espouses, which, in general terms, is in marked contrast to that of the Eastern Confucian traditions of collectivist conformity (Craft 2005).

Our definition of creativity in the context of the secondary school classroom is, therefore, going to be multi-faceted and complex and more of a contribution to the ongoing discussion than something definitive; more of a starting point than a finishing point in that discussion.

Towards a definition of critical thinking

When examining some of the literature on the current ideas surrounding 'critical thinking' we become conscious that this term is also open to a wide range of interpretations. Undeniably it is a complex and contested construct (Halpern 1998) and, like creativity, it is neither culturally nor politically neutral and is the core process of transformative learning. It is part cognitive skill set, part competence, part disposition, and we find that a number of writers see the value of effective critical thinking as being firmly rooted in the Western concept of what it is to be a contributing, participating member of society (Craft 2005; ten Dam and Volman 2004). The teaching of critical thinking could therefore be seen as a necessary part of education for 'critical' democratic citizenship, a required 'citizenship competence' (ten Dam and Volman 2004) and an essential part of citizenship education (DCSF 2007), as well as being part of the cognitive skill set needed for competence in higher-order thinking. Matthew Lipman (1991) and Robert Fisher (2005) share this view. Lipman, the creator of Philosophy for Children, describes critical thinking as being 'rational deliberation relevant to a democratic society' (1991; cited in ten Dam and Volman 2004: 361), while Robert Ennis describes it as 'reasonable reflective thinking that is focused on deciding what to believe or do' (1991b: 474). Michael Scriven and Richard Paul's (2003) definition of critical thinking goes like this: 'Critical thinking is the intellectually disciplined process of actively and skilfully conceptualizing, applying, analyzing, synthesizing, and/or evaluating information gathered from, or generated by, observation, experience, reflection, reasoning, or communication, as a guide to belief and action'.

A variety of ways of describing thinking in the context of learning have been developed over the years with attempts made to define different kinds of thinking. Benjamin Bloom (Bloom and Krathwohl 1956) saw three domains of educational activity: cognitive (to do with knowledge), affective (to do with attitude) and psychomotor (to do with skills). From the cognitive domain was developed the widely used hierarchical taxonomy of skills, comprising knowledge, comprehension and critical thinking, whence we get the notion of higher- and lower-order thinking skills. The year 1977 saw Gagné's proposal of the 'Five Learned Capabilities': intellectual skills, cognitive strategies, verbal information, attitudes and motor skills. One of the key values of this idea is its ability to distinguish between abstract and concrete definitions of learning. The thinking skills taxonomy developed by Swartz and Park (1994) is often seen as being more useful than Bloom's because of its greater detail and its non-hierarchical arrangement, and certainly the detail that it goes into is illuminating and could be very useful for teachers approaching the issues raised by this chapter as they look for access points that would enable them to develop their planning in thinking terms. More recently Anderson and Krathwohl's taxonomy (2001) has sought to modify Bloom by, among other adjustments, putting creativity (and the associated skills of planning, generating and producing) at the head of the list.

A consideration of the elements comprising Bloom's hierarchical taxonomy of learning domains – knowledge, comprehension, inference, application, analysis, synthesis and evaluation – can provide a useful starting point for our consideration of the concept of critical thinking. These six learning domains are described by Jennifer Moon (2008) as the 'tools for the manipulation of knowledge' and therefore very valuable when teasing out the different components of critical thinking. As we look at the skills of application, synthesis and evaluation, we see elements that suggest an ability to find and to solve problems, and elements of evaluation and judgement, and there is an implication that the critical thinking process takes time, energy and a high level of concentration. We have to conclude that there is a discrete skill set associated with critical thinking that has to be learned and that also includes elements of reflection and metacognition as pointed out by Diane Halpern: 'Critical thinking … involves evaluating the thinking process – the reasoning that went into the conclusion we've arrived at or the kinds of factors considered in making a decision' (2003: 7).

The skills usually associated with critical thinking, often called 'thinking skills', but more usefully referred to as features of critical awareness, are considered to be:

- the ability to analyse complex issues and problems;
- the recognition of different points of view and assumptions;
- the skill of evaluating these against a range of accepted criteria;
- being able to make inferences and draw conclusions based on available information;
- the ability to transfer these skills across subject boundaries;
- being able to see the interconnectedness of ideas and insights.

This could seem a daunting list. How can the practice of these skills be incorporated into the everyday classroom? Are these not skills that would be beyond many learners? The answers to these questions can be found in some of the techniques mentioned in Chapter 7. In the case of critical thinking the use of the 'community of enquiry' approach is one way of developing not only the skills of critical thinking among learners but also the motivation and the self-discipline that is needed. Such techniques as Philosophy for Children (P4C) and Mantle of the Expert (MoE) have been designed to provide support for both learner and teacher in carrying out enquiries that develop the use of critical thinking faculties at the appropriate level.

Teaching as creative enterprise

General creativity is a complex human mental process manifested to some degree in the dispositions and products of all individuals and groups. It is seen in the problem solving of everyday life, it is the spark that drives learning. It is susceptible to the features of the physical, intellectual and cultural environment and can be developed and nurtured, or indeed stifled, by these. In Western liberal democratic society it is seen as the driver of self-actualisation leading to the development of economic and social progress.

Creativity is, therefore, at the heart of good learning and teaching; the whole multi-directional social enterprise that takes place between learner and learner, learner and teacher is a creative process based on the growing facility of the learner's language and the way the teacher's understanding of this enables the creation of a learning environment that is promoting and nurturing of rich language. Creativity is inextricably associated with critical thinking; they are interrelated processes.

In the classroom where creative learning and teaching takes place we see evidence of a variety of features. There is a profusion of ideas and those ideas are celebrated fully in the shared learning space; there is evidence of richness in the use of language by both teachers and learners and that language is used to generate, elaborate and share ideas, speculate, hypothesise, experiment and wonder. Imagination is valued and there is evidence of cooperation, collaboration and sharing, and of support and the mutual respect of a variety of opinions. In a creative classroom there is always the possibility of synergy, there is always the possibility of something special happening. The key to this is the quality of the environment and it is easier, according to Csikszentmihalyi (1996), to enhance creativity by changing conditions in the environment than by trying to make people think more creatively.

It is easy to misinterpret the word creativity in the context of the classroom and the learning that goes on there. For some people that misinterpretation sends shudders down their collective spine as they imagine ungoverned learners being allowed to express themselves in disorganised and random ways. The pursuit of creativity seems to be a cover-up for bad and unruly behaviour, clearly indicative of disorganised thinking, unfocused learning and an at least tacit promotion of an attitude of general non-compliance. Edward de Bono (1992), however, makes the point that creativity is very serious and to imagine that it is just brainstorming and coming up with unfocused ideas is to show a deep misunderstanding of the issue. Robert Fisher (2005) lists four common misconceptions about creativity: that it is unrelated to critical thinking; that it is found in some subjects but not others; that creativity is simply doing your own thing; and that creativity requires a high IQ, and there are still those who regard creativity as being more to do with art, music and literature than to do with maths and science and the humanities. There are examples later in this book that show how a creative approach will enhance the learning in a range of subject areas and not all are necessarily considered arts areas.

Teaching itself is a creative enterprise and the creativity of the teacher is applicable in any subject; it is a combination of generic skills that need to be developed and consciously crafted over time. In Chapter 3 Best and Thomas propose that the creative process is common to all areas of human endeavour and can be understood through a Creativity Cycle comprising eight distinct steps. Creativity has a place in all aspects of the planning, construction and delivery of learning opportunities, but broader than that, it has to be part of the ethos of the school and woven into all aspects of the school's life. *All Our Futures* (1999), the NACCCE report to the Blair government on creativity in schools, inextricably binds creativity with cultural education and takes a holistic view, seeing it as being necessary to balance creative and cultural education. This, the report suggests, is to be achieved by means of the development of a 'systematic strategy' by a school that takes into account the curriculum, the pedagogies used and the means of assessing learning, as well as the need for a strong and dynamic relationship between the school and the wider community. There is also the recognition of the implications for resources for in-service training and staff development as, in recommendation 36, we see the suggestion that funding should be made available for priority in-service development and support of 'creative teaching and learning; creative thinking skills; the arts and humanities; teaching for cultural understanding' (NACCCE 1999: 200)

The use of creative techniques capable of promoting and developing critical thinking is necessary for learners of all abilities. Learners thrive when given cognitive challenges and when allowed space, time and the right environment to take up these challenges and think for themselves. At its root this issue is about how effectively teachers equip all their charges with the necessary life-skill tools. It is a rights and responsibilities issue and very much to do with how learners view themselves and how they understand their role in society and the sociocultural route that they need to take to get there. There are a number of methodologies that explicitly promote critical thinking techniques and provide teachers with procedural guidance and learners with structure, stimulus and challenge to move towards group solutions to problems and decision making. A compendium of these tools of the trade, as it were, of the creative teacher is given in Appendix 1 and there is a summary of each of these approaches in Chapter 7 along with links to resources and support.

Infusion or immersion?

It is not hard to see the core status of the skills associated with creative and critical thinking and, further, to realise that a teacher's understanding of them is essential, carrying with them very clear implications for the design of learning in terms both of procedure and process. The discussion that needs to be had is about whether these skills should be taught in a non-explicit way through the delivery of the curriculum – the 'immersion' method; or taught explicitly across the curriculum – the 'infusion' method. 'Infusion takes place when critical thinking principles are somehow made explicit' in the course of teaching curriculum subjects (Ennis 1997: 1). Should these skills be taught, then, or allowed to be caught? In the case of immersion, research has questioned whether the thinking skills practised in one curricular area are transferred either into other areas of learning or into the situations of everyday life. Marin and Halpern (2010) found that learners, both high and low achievers, benefited most from explicit instruction and repeated practice. In the report on the ACTS (Activating Children's Thinking Skills) project (2000), Carol McGuinness also supports infusion. In this research the rationale was that, if learners are to gain the skills of thinking flexibly and making reasoned judgements, this cannot be left to chance. Consequently, in the ACTS project curricular topics were identified and lessons were devised that allowed curricular objectives and thinking skills (based on the Swartz and Park taxonomy (1994)) to be simultaneously and explicitly pursued (McGuinness 2000). It is suggested by both Sternberg (1999) and Ennis (1991a, 1997) that a mixed approach could be the way forward in most situations, where both explicit and implicit methods are used deliberately and thoughtfully across the curriculum, and here lies the major implication for schools.

Thinking Schools

In order for learners to improve their critical thinking there does need to be a major change (Halpern 1998) in the way the teaching and learning process is viewed. Not only do we need a development in the mindset of teachers, a growth in the understanding of the importance of these skills for learners, but there needs also to be a development in the teachers' confidence in applying this understanding to the practice of the classroom. Use of infusion techniques does demand a degree of explicit teacher knowledge and so there are implications for the initial training and continued professional development of teachers. The objective would be to create thinking schools, thinking classrooms and a thinking curriculum as envisaged by McGuinness (2000).

As discussed earlier, the changes that have taken place in the relative positions of teachers and learners are indicative of something more than just social changes. These changes show the impact of developments that have taken place in the understanding of the learning process and also show that there needs to be a reappraisal of what actually happens in the classroom – how the interactions and transactions of learning take place, as well as what should constitute curricular content and how learning should be assessed. Here is a paradigm shift that says something about a move towards a particular vision of the classroom process that is focused more on how learners learn than how teachers teach. Schools in which such a reappraisal has taken place are different; the way they talk about them-selves and describe what they do is different; they have the self-confidence to talk explicitly about the learning and teaching that takes place rather than simply describe the syllabi used; there are structural differences in the ways that learning is viewed and organised and the observer can see a richness in the learning diet across and beyond the curriculum with links into the wider community. But, most importantly, it is possible to see the philosophical roots of the thinking behind the shared ethos that runs through the entire establishment.

The University of Exeter's web page 'Becoming a Thinking School' has the following definition:

> A Thinking School is an educational community in which all members share a common commitment to giving regular careful thought to every-thing that takes place. This will involve both students and staff learning how to think reflectively, critically and creatively, and employing these skills and techniques in the co-construction of a meaningful curriculum and associ-ated activities.

> (Burden 2006)

This clearly demonstrates the position that the schools already accredited by Exeter as Thinking Schools (55 Thinking Schools including five Advanced Thinking Schools, covering between them each of the key stages) have taken on learning and teaching. If we ponder but briefly on Paulo Freire's (2003) asser-tion that 'education … is an act of knowing rather than memorising', we realise that the way learning and teaching are conducted has to be different if we are to be successful in our objectives of guiding learners towards the acquisition, the development and the effective practice of the skills and attributes mentioned above.

Summary

From the foregoing it will be clear that the contributors of this book are taking a particular stance in relation to core issues surrounding creativity, critical thinking and the relationship that these concepts have with learning and teaching. There is an understanding of the different relationships and the changing social dynamics of the learning experience that are formed when creative approaches are taken and there is an understanding that these factors can generate transformational learning experiences. There is also the underlying understanding that there is a need for change if the work of schools is to be more effective in promoting among learners the aptitudes and attitudes that are necessary for a successful life in the twenty-first century.

Creativity is …

'The application of knowledge and skills in new ways, to achieve values and outcomes' (NCSL, cited in Eltecs n.d.) or, to put it another way, it is 'imaginative activity fashioned so as to produce outcomes that are both original and of value.' (NAACE, cited in Eltecs n.d.) and creativity thrives when it is identified, encouraged and fostered. The key features of creativity in both learners and teachers are: the use of the imagination, the pursuit of purposes, being original and judging value.

Critical thinking is …

A complex mixture of personal attributes, cognitive and social skills that will, given the right encouragement, grow in sophistication and effectiveness over time. In varying proportions the elements of critical awareness are: rationality, self-awareness, honesty, open-mindedness, discipline and judgement.

Critical thinkers …

Show critical awareness in that they are questioning, active and open-minded, they are analytical and capable of making evaluations, comparisons and balanced judgements, and they are organised and non-egotistical.

Creativity and critical thinking are very closely related and work together; they can be seen as two sides of the same coin. In the classroom there needs to be an awareness of the features, functions and power of each. Part of the dialogue in the creative classroom is about the understanding of how each type of thinking is working for both the learner and the teacher.

Discussion points

- What effect does an understanding of creativity and critical thinking have on the teachers' understanding of learning and teaching processes?
- What effects can this understanding have on the transactions of the classroom?
- What are the benefits for learners of a constructivist classroom?

Useful websites/resources

http://education.exeter.ac.uk/projects.php?id=29 Information on the Thinking School organisation.

www.criticalthinking.org/University/univclass/Defining.html *Defining Critical Thinking* by Scriven and Paul.

www.debonofoundation.co.uk Edward de Bono's thoughts and techniques.

References

Alexander, R. (2004) *Towards Dialogic Teaching: Rethinking classroom talk*, York: Dialogos.

Anderson, L. and Krathwohl, D.A. (2001) *Taxonomy for Learning, Teaching and Assessing: A revision of Bloom's Taxonomy of Educational Objectives*, New York: Longman.

Aronowitz, S. (1998) 'Introduction', in Freire, P., *Pedagogy of Freedom*, Lanham, MD: Rowman and Littlefield.

Bloom, B. and Krathwohl, D.R. (1956) *Taxonomy of Educational Objectives. Handbook 1: Cognitive Domain*, New York: David McKay.

Burden, R. (2006) *Becoming a Thinking School*. Available online at http://education.exeter. ac.uk/projects.php?id=29 (accessed 21 September 2011).

Carter, R. (2004) *Language and Creativity*, London: Routledge.

Claxton, G., Craft, A. and Gardner, H. (2008) (eds) *Creativity, Wisdom and Trusteeship*, Thousand Oaks, CA: Corwin Press.

Craft, A. (2003) 'The limits to creativity in education: dilemmas for the educator', *British Journal of Educational Studies*, 51(2): 113–27.

Craft, A. (2005) *Creativity in Schools: Tensions and dilemmas*, Oxford: Routledge.

Cropley, A.J. (1999) 'Creativity and cognition: producing effective novelty', *Roeper Review*, 21(4): 253–60.

Cropley, A.J. (2001) *Creativity in Education and Learning*, Oxford: Routledge.

Cropley, A.J. (2006) 'Creativity: a social approach', *Roeper Review*, 28(3): 125.

Csikszentmihalyi, M. (1996) *Creativity*, New York: Harper Perennial.

de Bono, E. (1992) *Serious Creativity*. Available online at www.debonogroup.com/ serious_creativity.php (accessed 28 October 2010).

Department for Children, Schools and Families (DCSF) (2007) *Citizenship: Programme of study for Key Stage 3*, London: DCSF.

Eltecs, J. (no date) *Teaching Creativity and Teaching for Creativity*. Available online at www. britishcouncil.org/jordan-eltecs-creativity.ppt (accessed 31 July 2012).

Ennis, R.H. (1991a) 'Critical thinking: a streamlined conception', *Teaching Philosophy*, 14(1): 5–25.

Ennis, R.H. (1991b) 'Discrete thinking skills in two teachers' physical education classes', *Elementary School Journal*, 91(5): 473–87. Made available courtesy of the University of Chicago Press, www.press.uchicago.edu.

Ennis, R.H. (1997) 'Incorporating critical thinking in the curriculum: an introduction to some basic issues', *Inquiry: Critical Thinking Across the Disciplines*, 16(3): 1–9.

Feist, G.R. (1999) 'The influence of personality on artistic and scientific creativity', in Sternberg, R.J. (ed.) *Handbook of Creativity*, New York: Cambridge University Press.

Freire, P. (1998) *Pedagogy of Freedom*, Lanham, MD: Rowman and Littlefield.

Freire, P. (2003) *Cultural Action for Freedom*, Harmondsworth: Penguin.

Fisher, R. (2005) *Teaching Children to Think* (2nd edn), London: Nelson Thornes.

Guilford, J.P. (1950) 'Creativity', *American Psychologist*, 5: 444–54.

Gornall, S., Chambers, M. and Claxton, G. (2005) *Building Learning Power in Action*, Bristol: TLO.

Halpern, D.F. (1998) 'Teaching critical thinking for transfer across domains: dispositions, skills, structure training, and metacognitive monitoring', *American Psychologist*, 53: 449–55.

Halpern, D.F. (2003) *Thought and Knowledge: An introduction to critical thinking*, Mahwah, NJ: Lawrence Erlbaum.

Halpern, D.F. (2005) *Thought and Knowledge* (4th edn), Mahwah, NJ: Lawrence Erlbaum.

King, A. (1993) 'From sage on the stage to guide on the side', *College Teaching*, 41(1): 30–5.

Lipman, M. (1991) *Thinking in Education*, Cambridge: Cambridge University Press.

McGuinness, C. (2000) 'ACTS: a methodology for teaching thinking across the curriculum', *Teaching Thinking*, 2: 1–12.

Marin, L.M. and Halpern, D.F. (2010) 'Pedagogy for developing critical thinking in adolescents: explicit instruction produces greatest gains', *Thinking Skills and Creativity*: Doi: 10.1016/j.tsc.2010.08.002.

Mayer, R.E. (1999) 'Fifty years of creativity research', in Sternberg, R.J. (ed.) *Handbook of Creativity*, New York: Cambridge University Press, pp. 449–60.

Mercer, N. (2006) *The Guided Construction of Knowledge*, Clevedon: Multilingual Matters.

Moon, J. (2008) *Critical Thinking*, Oxford: Routledge.

National Advisory Committee on Creative and Cultural Education (NACCCE) (1999) *All Our Futures: Creativity, culture and education* (The Robinson Report), London: HMSO.

Nickerson, R.S. (1999) 'Enhancing creativity', in Sternberg, R.J. (ed.) *Handbook of Creativity*, New York: Cambridge University Press.

Qualifications and Curriculum Authority (QCA) (2007) *Citizenship Programme of Study for Key Stage 3 and Attainment Targets*, London: QCA.

Scriven, M. and Paul, R. (2003) *Defining Critical Thinking*. Available online at www.criticalthinking.org/University/univclass/Defining.html (accessed 10 January 2012).

Sternberg, R.J. (ed.) *Handbook of Creativity*, New York: Cambridge University Press.

Swartz, R. and Parks, S. (1994) *Infusing the Teaching of Critical and Creative Thinking into Content Instruction*, Pacific Grove, CA: Critical Thinking Press.

ten Dam, G. and Volman, M. (2004) 'Critical thinking as a citizenship competence: teaching strategies', *Learning and Instruction*, 14: 359–79.

Willis, J. (2009) 'Assessment for learning: a sociocultural approach', in Jeffery, P. (ed.) *Proceedings of Changing Climates: Education for sustainable futures*, Australian Association for Research in Education, 30 November–4 December 2008, Kelvin Grove, Queensland.

2

Creativity in – creativity out

Creativity and critical thinking in the context of initial teacher training

Steve Padget

Key questions

- What are the personal attributes that teachers need to bring with them and develop actively as essential components of their professional practice?

- What bearing does an understanding of teacher and learner language have on the notions of creativity and critical thinking and the learning transactions of the classroom?

- What are the essentials of a creative learning plan?

Setting the scene

The purpose of this chapter is to examine some of the key ideas that lead us to an understanding of the importance of creativity and the role it plays in the processes of learning and teaching. At the head of the chapter are three key questions that teachers, those in training, those newly qualified and those with years of experience behind them should be asking themselves. The quest for the answers to these questions will guide the teacher to affirm that there are personal qualities needed to be a successful and effective teacher as well as philosophical, ethical, intellectual and professional understandings.

The relationship between creativity, education and learning can be viewed at two levels: first, the macro level, where creativity is seen as being a major driver of current national education policies across large parts of the world; and, second, the micro level, where we need to examine how notions of creativity influence pedagogic practice. This chapter has its focus more on pedagogy than sociopolitics and looks at the implications an understanding of creativity has for the shape of learning in a school setting.

In Chapter 1 the idea was articulated that we all possess some measure of creativity – small 'c' creativity (Craft 2002), which is part of that range of personal attributes, attitudes and dispositions that we bring to bear on the day-to-day situations that we encounter; it is the problem solving of life and it is the medium of learning. We now need to look further into how an understanding of this should inform the effective teacher and how it is essential that small 'c' creativity is brought into the classroom along with the other qualities and motivations. Creativity, of both teacher and learner, is a state of mind, and like all brain-based functions it is difficult to define, ethereal and elusive (Berggraf Saebø *et al.* 2007), and the ways in which it can manifest itself in the context of day-to-day classroom work are many and various and include the development in all learners of the capacity for critical thought.

Definitions

The terms 'creativity' and 'critical thinking' have been defined in many ways, but for the purposes of clarity in this chapter the definitions iterated in Chapter 1 can be recalled.

Creativity is:

- 'the application of knowledge and skills in new ways, to achieve values and outcomes' (NCSL, cited in Eltecs n.d.);

- 'imaginative activity fashioned so as to produce outcomes that are both original and of value' (NAACE, cited in Eltecs n.d.).

The features of creativity are:

- the use of the imagination, the pursuit of purposes, being original and judging value;
- creativity thrives when it is identified, encouraged and fostered.

Critical thinking is:

- a complex mixture of personal skills which will, given the right encouragement, grow in sophistication and effectiveness over time. In varying proportions these skills are: rationality, self-awareness, honesty, open-mindedness, discipline and judgement or, in other words, the ability to make evaluations against appropriate criteria. These are the 'thinking skills' that have been categorised by many writers as those of the 'higher order' to contrast them with the 'lower-order' skills of remembering, understanding and applying as seen in Bloom's hierarchical taxonomy (Bloom and Krathwohl 1956). Critical thinking can be said to be one of the key objectives of education and Halpern's shorthand version of the definition is as succinct as it is illuminating:

> Attitude + Knowledge + Thinking Skills = Intelligent Thinking.
> (Halpern 2003: 7; after Russell via d'Angelo)

The relationship between creativity and critical thinking is close, almost symbiotic, inasmuch as creativity needs the ground that is prepared by critical thinking in which to grow. One of the principal outcomes, therefore, of creative teaching is a growing facility in learners to make appropriate and informed critical judgements that will be seen as well-grounded evaluations of relative worth as applied to their decisions, their actions and all the elements of the sea of stimuli in which they exist. This is seen by some researchers as being one of the essential skills needed to participate effectively in today's society – 'If education is to further the critical competence of students, it must provide them with the opportunity at the level of the classroom and the school to observe, imitate and practice critical agency and to reflect upon it' (ten Dam and Volman 2004).

Developing a personal philosophy

If schools are to value appropriately, nurture effectively and harness constructively the creativity of their learners, those learners need to be guided by practitioners who possess a great deal of understanding of the importance of creativity. They also need to appreciate creativity as a component of the whole landscape of learning and this has to be reflected in both the content and the philosophical cast of training programmes. Responsibility for the development of this understanding is therefore divided between the teacher training institution or graduate teacher consortium and the school, giving school-based mentors a great deal of this weight. As the current modes of postgraduate teacher training have developed, the time available for taught sessions away from school has become increasingly squeezed. The onus now is upon the school to deliver effective input across a widening range of topics, the understanding of which is crucial to the effective development of the new teacher.

While the apprenticeship model is to be commended for many things, it leaves the trainee with much necessary self-study in some very important areas of understanding. There is a risk that the trainee will complete the programme being strong on day-to-day tactics but with a relatively underdeveloped grasp of the importance of a philosophically based strategic overview that is needed to inform both purpose and methodology. Successful performance in the classroom depends upon the acquisition of many skills, but it is underpinned by a clear working philosophy, even if that appears to be somewhat below the surface in the case of many busy teachers in the context of their day-to-day classroom and school responsibilities. The education of teachers is more than merely training in technique – it is rooted in the formation of the ethical self (Freire 1998) and the trainee will quickly realise that their journey towards success in the profession is one of personal discovery as well as professional development.

Philosophical development starts with the growing awareness of the child-centred nature of the learning process, with the appreciation of how close the relationship is between language, thought and learning, culture and society; that 'effective teaching is much more than just a compilation of skills and strategies [and] is a deliberate philosophical and ethical code of conduct' (Larrivee 2000: 294); and that the practising teacher is making 'a purposive cultural intervention in individual human development which is deeply saturated with the values and history of the society and community in which it is located' (Alexander 2005: 2).

At the outset of their learning journey aspirant teachers frequently and understandably recall, and initially at least are inclined to imitate, the models of learning and teaching with which they are familiar, based on their own experiences as school learners. This is reflected in the findings of recent research (Davies *et al.* 2004) and it is not confined to younger trainees on postgraduate courses. For some of the older EBITT (employment-based initial teacher training) trainees, those who are seeking career change, the models of learning and teaching that they recall can be markedly different from the current practice. All trainees embark upon the programme wanting to be teachers, wanting to teach their classes about the things that they know, those things that have provided them with their own life's stimulation and motivation, and they sometimes find it hard to make the necessary adjustment to their perception of how a creative teacher operates. Trainees are therefore to be encouraged to move away from the suggestion of a 'banking' concept of education, where the learners passively receive that which is owned by the teachers, filing and storing deposits of information (Freire 1970), towards a model of personal transformation that puts the learner at the centre of the picture, a model where teachers and learners are asking questions, solving problems, making connections and making meaning dialogically. Creative teachers realise the importance of knowing the situatedness of the learners; they guide rather than tell; they model learning and create possibilities for the construction of meaning rather than the dispensing of knowledge.

Those ITT programmes are to be applauded that enable trainees to explore their own creativity and come to terms with its potential for their own learning and that of learners. Trainees will benefit when they are given the opportunity to gain an understanding of the development of creativity in learners and an understanding of how this can be identified, encouraged and fostered. Craft (2000) emphasises the development of the relationship with self and others that is at the heart of creativity and that this can only take place in a 'self-knowing' training programme. For this to happen there needs to be emotional support, a coherent and supportive trainee network, and the opportunity in the structure of the programme for trainees to receive effective feedback that is away from, but linked to, their learning and teaching situation (Craft 2000). The importance of the personal development that takes place during the programme cannot be overstated and for many it is profoundly life-changing.

The particular attributes of trainees that are scrutinised and actively developed in training and beyond are:

- a commitment to the development of their own and others' learning;
- a view of themselves as being creative individuals;
- a commitment to sharing ideas;
- an open-mindedness to innovation and flexibility of approach.

To these, as the training progresses, will be added professional, technical and ethical understandings, including:

- a developing concept of the term 'creativity', taking it from a narrow arts- and performance-based concept to an appreciation of the broader implications of creativity in the context of the learning and teaching experience;
- an appreciation of the close relationship that exists between creativity and critical thinking;
- a rapidly growing repertoire of creative teaching strategies with the confidence, understanding and ability to deliver them;
- an awareness of the distinctive dynamics of the creative classroom;
- an explicit understanding of the centrality of language in the thinking and learning process and the implications of this;
- the ability to reflect critically in order to grow professionally and learn from experience.

A coherent personal philosophy of learning and teaching will develop as depth of understanding increases with experience. The details of this will be informed by active, detailed and insightful observation, planning and classroom practice and well-directed reading. Teaching for creative learning and the development of critical thinking demands that we look at the learning process in a constructivist way, where:

- the learner is placed at the centre of the learning process;

- curricular arrangements are developed to suit the learners' prior knowledge;

- learning is based on searching for and making meaning and problem solving in a dynamic social setting;

- methods are used that enable learners to make new connections, thereby gaining new understandings;

- there is an expectation that learners' analyses, interpretations and hypotheses will be valued as key steps of learning, thus promoting critical thinking skills;

- the language life is democratic and rich with dialogic transactions based on the use of open, rich and provocative questions;

- learners learn how to take part in the assessment of their progress;

- and, fundamentally, where the activity of teaching is not the transfer of knowledge, but the creation of possibilities for the construction of knowledge (Freire 1998: 30).

Creativity and learning

The nature of creativity and its relationship with learning have been discussed widely and vigorously, and the value of this discussion is that it has served to focus much attention on the nature of learning. This has taken place in the context of the rapidly developing understanding in neuroscience and in the psychology of learning as well as the development of sociocultural and social constructivist approaches to learning in particular. This has resulted in the existence of a much more focused and coherent literature than was the case in the recent past, when much of what existed was the result of the drive to develop simple behaviourist theories (John-Steiner 1996). From the sociocultural perspective we need to examine the range of opportunities that learners must be given for meaning making by using imaginative and inclusive pedagogies that involve, among other things, the appropriate scaffolding of learners' efforts and the modelling of teacher disposition (Craft et al. 2007). The creativity of the teacher is then brought to bear on the ways in which these, and the growing capacity for critical thought, become the weft and warp of the learning experience.

The visible products in the classroom that are a function of creativity can be seen in, for example, the ways that problems have been solved and the quality of both the conclusions arrived at and of the decision-making process itself. There is richness in the thinking activities and the beneficial effects on the learning can be seen. There are some subtle understandings present that will make the experience of the learners more inclusive, more dynamic, more purposeful, more collaborative and more effective, with enhanced cognition and metacognition.

Much research has concluded that the benefits of encouraging and facilitating creativity are many in terms of personal development and the growth in learners' capabilities. Pupils who are encouraged to think creatively and independently become more interested in discovering new things for themselves, more open to new ideas, keener to work with others to explore ideas, and more willing to work beyond lesson time when pursuing an idea or a vision. As a result of this, it has been discovered, their pace of learning, levels of achievement and self-esteem all increase (NACCCE 1999). Positive dispositions, while they may already exist to varying degrees in the make-up of learners, have to be dynamically nurtured and encouraged, and this development cannot be left to chance. *All Our Futures* (NACCCE 1999: 95) proposes the need for teachers to be mindful of three key issues:

- The need for the teacher to be adept at *identifying* creativity both in themselves and in the learners. Teachers should be looking for creative, imaginative and stimulating possibilities in the planning and the structuring of learning; they need to develop the ability to recognise and acknowledge the value in pupils' utterances, responses and products of learning and to be able to respond appropriately.

- The importance of being able to *encourage* creativity in learners by allowing them to feel comfortable in taking chances and in seeing new possibilities. This needs to come from the teacher's own enthusiasm, their depth of subject knowledge, the fact that their presence in the classroom models a creative outlook that is manifested in the methodologies used, and the understanding of the power and purpose of these and the value of the resultant climate that is created in the class.

- The importance of *fostering* creativity in learners. Creativity generates creativity and just as this should be modelled by the teacher it should also be understood by the learners that they can learn from each other. This can only be done by considering actively the class arrangements – groupings, physical layout, the management of learning – and this implies a clear understanding of why the particular arrangements have been chosen. Within the structure of these arrangements is the need for the feeling of learner inclusivity to be infused in the class where everyone, including the teacher, is a co-participator, a co-creator, and part of a joint endeavour (Craft 2005).

The creative classroom

When we plan for learning that encourages critical thinking we are ourselves thinking creatively. The essence of critical thinking is a questioning and challenging approach to knowledge and Harrington (1990) lists a number of components that need to be present in a creative classroom that will allow for critical thinking to take place and describes what he calls the 'creative ecosystem', which, he suggests, consists of the following interrelated elements:

- opportunity for play and experimentation/exploration;
- a non-threatening atmosphere in which learners are secure enough to take risks and make mistakes;
- activities presented in exciting or unusual contexts;
- opportunity for generative thought, where ideas are greeted openly;
- opportunity for critical reflection in a supportive environment;
- children given a sense of engagement and ownership of ideas and tasks;
- respect for difference and the creativity of others;
- choices given to children in terms of resources and methods.

Each of these features makes important assumptions about the role and position of the teacher, about the nature of the thinking and the activity of the learners, and about the quality of the relationships that exist in that space, all of which are transcendent of the curricular subject. The 'creative ecosystem' shows a clear recognition of the essentially social and collaborative nature of effective learning that contrasts markedly with didactic, transmission models of learning and teaching, which only emphasise the worth of the individual's solo achievements.

The successfully creative classroom is, therefore, a function of certain inter-connected understandings. There is the presence of a learner-centred model of learning and teaching with an understanding of the implications and expectations that this has for the teacher–learner relationship. There is an understanding in this of the essentially dialogic nature of effective learning and the power and the value of talk, to, with, by and between learners. There is the understanding that this talk cannot take place in a vacuum and arrangements made must facilitate this to create the desired creative climate.

One of the essential developmental skills of the teacher is the increasing ability to choose from a range of appropriate strategies and approaches over the course of time; good classrooms are places of flexibility and are responsive to learners' needs. The creative climate alone is not enough and the teacher's role must be seen as going beyond simply being an encouraging adult and must embrace specific active techniques and strategies (NGfL Scotland 2003). Chapter 7 provides an overview of key creative learning and teaching techniques that incorporate the collaborative use of language in child-centred, meaning-making and problem-solving approaches. These are further summarised with references to principal works and authors in Appendix 1.

'Creative teaching is seen to involve teachers in making learning more interesting and effective and using imaginative approaches in the classroom' (Cremin 2009: 36). Learning can take place anywhere and we are all aware of the power of the learning environment that is in itself stimulating by being unusual and unconventional perhaps; farms, zoos, playgrounds, fields, woods and so forth are all places where rich learning can take place. And the activities for learning can be equally varied, be they digging in ruins, or collecting leaves in forests or shells from beaches. However, as these situations do not provide the most usual day-to-day learning environment, being based in the prosaic surroundings of most classrooms, something has to be done to enliven and enhance and invigorate the learning space.

The physical nature of the learning space with its advantages and limitations is one thing; the décor of the room can be enhanced in enlivening and stimulating ways but walls, after all, are walls, and no amount of will-power on the part of the teacher can alter that fact. However, there are more subtle creators of environment under the control of the creative teacher. Based on the understanding that learning is a social enterprise and that how the teacher relates to the learners and how the learners relate to one another are the essential dynamics of the process, there are things that the creative teacher needs to address in the construction of a space where there is exploration, where there can be enquiry, where there is stimulation and where there is support.

The creative classroom is a safe space, a place where:

- there is questioning and challenge;
- there is the opportunity to make new connections and see new relationships;
- learners are able to envisage what might be;
- there is the exploration of ideas and the options are kept open;
- there is the mental space to reflect critically on ideas, actions and outcomes;
- there is the expectation that all are involved;
- there is support for and value given to each learner's efforts.

Language and creative teaching

The nature of the learning transactions that take place in classrooms has changed considerably over time. Pedagogic approaches that were considered appropriate in the second half of the twentieth century are being replaced as the research-based understanding of the learning process has been deepened and refined, and as political and cultural shifts have impacted upon the work of the classroom. But the informed observer might also see the resistance to change that certain transmission models of teaching show. There still seems to be a measure of reluctance in some classrooms to embrace a more democratic, more egalitarian form of teacher–learner discourse, one that is built upon an understanding of the power of the active use of language. Wolfe and Alexander (2008) see this, and the slow speed of change, as being evidence of the dilemma faced by teachers as they grapple with the implications of the growing research-based evidence pointing to the need to allow learners 'to reason, argue and adopt the habits of critical enquiry'. The implication, they suggest, is that changes in the way that schools frame knowledge and assess learning are as essential as they are fundamental.

In order to teach creatively an understanding of the need for the measured use of language has to be manifest and the planning process needs to look imaginatively and in some little detail at the nature of language use that is going to take place in the lesson. The widespread acceptance of the Vygotskian understanding that effective verbal reasoning is a skill developed in a social setting leads us to examine the importance of both the social and the language dynamic of the lesson. What balance should there be between different language forms such as telling and explanation, questioning, discussion and dialogue? What are the different functions and values of these elements of the repertoire? The effective use of language is the bridge to the learner, and the teacher who knows this appreciates that language both manifests and structures thinking (Alexander 2005) and is the foundation of learning itself (Halliday 1993).

The principal architects of the current research into the impact of dialogue on learning and sociocultural theory are, respectively, Robin Alexander and Neil Mercer and their main texts are listed at the end of this chapter. Here is a body of scholarship that clearly articulates the theoretical base, the research evidence and the practical implications that arise when the principles of dialogic talk in the class are used to underpin pedagogy. Mercer (2000, reiterated in Mercer and Littleton 2007: 133) coined the term *interthinking*, to describe the talk used by learners to think collectively, thus linking the cognitive and social functions of group talk. Alexander (2004) describes the nature of the different kinds of talk in the classroom and, having analysed these, goes on to demonstrate how meaningful dialogic talk can be achieved. Both these eminent academics have conducted extensive research over a number of years and have agreed with Vygotsky's claim that social interaction does in fact shape intellectual development through the medium of language, the main human cultural tool.

For classroom talk to be dialogic it must have certain features: it must be collective, reciprocal, supportive and also cumulative and purposeful (Alexander 2004). It is collective because it is a social process; reciprocal because listening and responsive contributions take place; and supportive in the way utterances are received with linguistic and paralinguistic signals and reactions. It is also cumulative and purposeful because utterances in response to questions move over time from being right or wrong to being cognitive stepping stones and the talk builds and moves towards planned purposes (Alexander 2004). The planned use of language therefore defines the learning that is going to take place in the class and there are features enabling of creative dialogue that need to be present. Fisher (2009) mentions 12 key features that need to be considered. These can be used to interrogate planning and, bearing in mind that not all 12 features need to be present in each lesson, over a period of time it would be useful to reflect on whether the teaching and learning that was being planned was including them collectively, in combination and individually, as integral parts of the child-centred pedagogies being habitually used.

According to Fisher (2009: 11), does the teaching allow for the following:

- Opportunities for learners to ask questions?
- A shared agenda?
- The use of imaginative and exploratory language?

- The encouragement of alternative viewpoints?
- The reflective use of dialogue?
- How does the use of language define the teacher–pupil relationship?
- Is persuasive language encouraged?
- Are there situations where a range of possible answers is expected, received and celebrated?
- Is language used as the medium of cooperative enquiry?
- Does the language used promote the personalisation of learning?
- Is the language used related to the inner purposes of the learners?
- The 'I–thou' relationship?

By looking at the language life of the classroom in a holistic way a potential can immediately be seen that makes the stultifying and much overused 'Initiation-Response-Evaluation' teacher/whole-class 'interaction' seem rather threadbare, lacking in cognitive effectiveness and loaded with negative and non-inclusive values. The ideas above allow us to think about the wide range of possibilities that exist.

The potential for a language-rich classroom becomes reality when the art of the teacher's questioning develops. This is necessary for the success of the learning and over time will develop into something sharply focused and powerful; deeper questions will lead to deeper enquiry. Meaningful arrangements of learners need to be used and the interactions between them need to be fostered, focused and managed. The teacher's feedback will become informative rather than merely encouraging; it will become a real part of the progress of the learning dialogue, not merely inquisitorial or just indulgently appreciative. Moreover, the teacher's questions will not be the only ones that are being addressed; learners will be framing and asking questions, responding and feeding back to each other – this is learning in the sociocultural round.

Creative planning for creative learning

From what has gone before it will be clear that the creative teacher is someone with a specific mindset able to see the importance of reflecting on questions about their teaching and about the relationship between that and creativity. They will have made the link between this and the encouragement and facilitation of critical thinking. They will have begun the process of working out what they believe to be the function and purpose of the teacher's role and the wider purpose of education. They will also be increasingly ready to see the impact that this understanding will have on planning, delivery, the methodologies selected and the techniques used at different points in the lesson in pursuit of the lesson's learning objectives. The Ofsted survey of creativity in schools concluded that:

teachers were seen to promote creative learning most purposefully and effectively when encouraging pupils to question and challenge, make connections and see relationships, speculate, keep options open while pursuing a line of enquiry, and reflect critically on ideas, actions and results.

(Ofsted 2010: 5–6)

Armed with the succinct definition that creativity is 'imaginative activity fashioned so as to produce outcomes that are both original and of value' (NACCCE 1999: 30) the planning process can begin. *All Our Futures* (NACCCE 1999) asks us to consider whether the teaching proposed in a lesson plan is going to be purposeful, original and valuable, and whether it involves the use of the imagination. It is useful to examine these issues more closely in terms of questions that trainees could usefully ask themselves; the parameters are: purpose, originality, value and exercising of the imagination.

Is the learning in this plan purposeful?

- Do you have ownership of the ideas? Will a freshness and a commitment to what you are doing come through?

- Has the learning plan aroused curiosity, emotion, interest and passion in you and is it, therefore, capable of arousing some of those feelings in the learners?

- Has there been some measure of co-construction and learner input, thereby showing a responsiveness to the learners' needs?

- Is the learning path and purpose clear and relevant to the learners and is there a clearly visible link between this work and what has gone before?

- Is the methodology chosen underpinned by the use of language and is it actively engaging, inclusive, cooperative and encouraging of a range of learner–teacher dynamics?

Is there a measure of originality?

- What elements of this plan are original – and how is this originality demonstrated, for example the use of unexpected questions, unusual challenges or unusual outcomes?

- What elements of the plan will allow for the originality of the learners' efforts to be stimulated and supported?

- How is the originality of the learning outcomes to be recognised in relation to work previously done?

- How is this achievement going to be celebrated?

Is the learning in this plan of value?

- Is it clear to you and the learners what the value of the learning contained in the plan will be in relation to its cognitive and metacognitive purpose?

- Is there an opportunity for you and the learners to critically appraise the achievements of the lesson and to share these appraisals?

Does this plan show imagination?

- Has a potentiating context been created, with an interesting environment, with unusual stimuli?

- Are there new ideas in the planning that can be enjoyed by both teacher and learners?

- Are there areas where the learners could be divergent and original, create unexpected responses and express alternative views and have them listened to?

- Is there a journey planned that will take the learners from the familiar into new territory?

Evidencing creativity

Through the active reflection contained in the self-evaluation of the lesson, the teacher will be able to make valuable assessment of the outcomes of the lesson against both the cognitive and metacognitive objectives. Valuable as this process is, it has to be seen in the context of the assessment of the teacher's performance and this raises the question of how the creativity in a lesson can be assessed. The issue here is whether the observer/assessor is appropriately briefed before the lesson and how well the documentation of the lesson is prepared; does this allow the observer to see a clear picture of the lesson's ethos and intentions (Robson *et al.* 2009)? Does the plan make sufficiently explicit the teacher's understanding of the relationship between language, thinking and learning? Is this understanding clear in the delivery of the lesson as well as in the planning?

The *Teachers' Standards* document (DfE 2011) does not mention creativity or critical thinking explicitly but subsumes these within the standards and subsidiary bullet points as with other details of the pedagogic approach. Teachers will be assessed on the effectiveness of their overall performance, the assumption being that high-quality components make a high-quality lesson. The expectation is that part of the effectiveness of the teaching will be the demonstrable facility in the use of creative and imaginative techniques. It is worth noting that, in the current Ofsted inspection framework, evidence of the use of creative teaching techniques, good questioning and the promotion of wide and deep thinking can be commented upon specifically. This can be taken as an indication of the importance that is being attached to these components of creative teaching, and the Ofsted report, *Learning: Creative approaches that raise standards*, shows how, since the ending of KS3 tests, schools have been able to exercise greater flexibility in the design of curricula to 'extend opportunities for creative and interactive approaches to learning' (Ofsted 2010: 4).

Appendix 2 shows where creativity and critical thinking will be most relevant as part of the assessment of achievement against the *Teachers' Standards*. Those standards are in bold italics where creativity and critical thinking can be part of the evidence of achievement. The responsibility lies with the trainee, therefore, to evidence explicitly the creative aspects of the lesson through annotations of the plan, to ensure that the methodologies adopted are suitable and to make sure that the observer/assessor is appropriately briefed, and, finally, to reflect in detail on the success of the lesson in terms of the creative methods used.

A very coherent and comprehensive guide to the practical issues of creativity in the classroom, along with planning resources designed for the teacher in training, can be found on the ESCalate website by following the link to the Creativity in Initial Teacher Education (CITE) project. The final chapter of this book gives details of a variety of creative teaching methodologies along with a summary of the approaches and references for further research and resources; these approaches are tabulated in Appendix 1. Details of examples of practical teaching ideas using a range of creative teaching techniques and promoting critical thinking can be found in a companion volume to this book, *Global Learning and Sustainable Development* (Padget and Pout 2011).

Key reading

On the strategic issues of creativity in learning and teaching:
Craft, A. (2005) *Creativity in Schools: Tensions and dilemmas*, Oxford: Routledge.
On language and dialogic classroom talk:
Alexander, R.J. (2004) *Towards Dialogic Teaching: Rethinking classroom talk* (4th edn), York: Dialogos.
On practical approaches to creative learning in the classroom:
Fisher, R. (2009) *Creative Dialogue: Talk for thinking in the classroom*, Oxford: Routledge.

Useful websites/resources

http://escalate.ac.uk/resources /The Higher Education Academy, Education Subject Centre advancing teacher education (ESCalate). Follow the link to the Creativity in Initial Teacher Education (CITE) project.

www.ltscotland.org.uk/creativity/ NGfL Scotland (2003) *Creativity in Education Online.*

References

Alexander, R.J. (2004) *Towards Dialogic Teaching: rethinking classroom talk* (4th edn), York: Dialogos.

Alexander, R.J. (2005) 'Education, culture and cognition: intervening for growth' Keynote presented at Culture, Dialogue and Learning: Notes on an emerging pedagogy, University of Cambridge, 12 July.

Berggraf Saebø, A., McCammon, L.A. and O'Farrell, L. (2007) 'Creative teaching – teaching creativity', *Caribbean Quarterly*, 53(1/2).

Bloom, B. and Krathwohl, D.R. (1956) *Taxonomy of Educational Objectives. Handbook 1: Cognitive domain*, New York: David McKay.

Craft, A. (2000) *Creativity Across the Primary Curriculum: Framing and developing practice*, London: Routledge.

Craft, A. (2002) *Creativity in the Early Years: A lifewide foundation*, London: Continuum.

Craft, A. (2005) *Creativity in Schools: Tensions and dilemmas*, Oxford: Routledge.

Craft, A., Cremin, T., Burnard, P. and Chappell, K. (2007) 'Teacher stance in creative learning: a study of progression', *Journal of Thinking Skills and Creativity*, 2(2): 136–47.

Cremin, T. (2009) 'Creative teachers and creative teaching', in Wilson, A. (ed.) *Creativity in Primary Education* (2nd edn), Exeter: Learning Matters, pp. 36–46.

Davies, D., Howe, A., Fasciato, M. and Rogers, M. (2004) 'How do trainee primary teachers understand creativity?' Paper presented at BERA Annual Conference, University of Manchester, September.

Department for Education (DfE) (2011) *Teachers' Standards*, London: Department for Education.

Eltecs, J. (no date) *Teaching Creativity and Teaching for Creativity*. Available online at www.britishcouncil.org/jordan-eltecs-creativity.ppt (accessed 31 July 2012).

Fisher, R. (2009) *Creative Dialogue: Talk for thinking in the classroom*, Oxford: Routledge.

Freire, P. (1970) *Pedagogy of the Oppressed* (translated from Portuguese by M. Bergman Ramos), London: Penguin Books, 1996.

Freire, P. (1998) *Pedagogy of Freedom* (translated from Portuguese by P. Clarke), Oxford: Rowman and Littlefield.

Halliday, M.A.K. (1993) 'Towards a language based theory of learning', *Linguistics in Education*, 5: 93–116.

Halpern, D. (2003) *Thought and Knowledge* (4th edn), Mahwah, NJ: Lawrence Erlbaum.

Harrington, D.M. (1990) 'The ecology of human creativity: a psychological perspective', in Runco, M.A. and Albert, R.S. (eds) *Theories of Creativity*, London: Sage.

John-Steiner, V. (1996) 'Creativity and collaboration in knowledge construction'. Paper presented at National Council of Teachers of English Assembly on Research. Vygotsky Centennial: Vygotskian perspectives on literacy and research, Chicago, IL.

Larrivee, B. (2000) 'Transforming teaching practice: becoming the critically reflective teacher', *Reflective Practice*, 1(3): 293–307.

Mercer, N. (2000) *Words and Minds: How we use language to think together*, London: Routledge.

Mercer, N. and Littleton, K. (2007) *Dialogue and the Development of Children's Thinking*, London: Routledge.

National Advisory Committee on Creative and Cultural Education (NACCCE) (1999) *All Our Futures: Creativity, culture and education* (The Robinson Report), London: HMSO.

National Grid for Learning (NGfL) Scotland 2003 *Creativity in Education*. Available online at www.ltscotland.org.uk/creativity (accessed 8 July 2011).

Ofsted (2010) *Learning: Creative approaches that raise standards*, Manchester: Ofsted.

Padget, S. and Pout, L. (2011) 'Classroom approaches' and 'Provocations', in Gadsby, H. and Bullivant, A. (eds) *Global Learning and Sustainable Development*, Oxford: Routledge.

Robson, C., Patterson, R. and Kidd, D. (2009) *Planning for Creativity in the Curriculum of Initial Teacher Education Programmes*, Manchester: Manchester Metropolitan University, Training and Development Agency for Schools.

ten Dam, G. and Volman, M. (2004) 'Critical thinking as a citizenship competence: teaching strategies', *Learning and Instruction*, 14: 359–79.

Wolfe, S. and Alexander, R. (2008) *Argumentation and Dialogic Teaching: Alternative pedagogies for a changing world*, London: DCSF, Beyond Current Horizons Project, Futurelab.

3

A framework for creativity in schools

Brin Best and Will Thomas

Key questions

- What specifically is creativity?
- What are the interrelationships between creativity and the way we access our thinking capabilities?
- How can creativity be applied to the current classroom situation in terms of learning, teaching and teacher performance?

In this chapter we will provide an overall framework for thinking about creativity in schools. We will explain the difference between creative teaching, creative learning and teaching for creativity and will explore the popular myths around creativity and the conditions needed for it to thrive. We will introduce the Creativity Cycle, our eight-step model for conceptualising the different stages in the creative process, and will explain how both teachers and pupils can use the cycle to increase their creativity and improve their learning. Our chapter will then go on to consider the role of creativity in the various domains of a teacher's work, and the need for leadership for creativity in schools. Throughout the chapter we will use concise case studies from schools to illuminate points made in the text.

Creativity makes us human

In September 2011, archaeologists announced that an unusual series of abstract cave 'paintings' had been found deep inside a complex subterranean system in the Dordogne, southwest France. What makes this discovery particularly significant is that the primitive works of art – dated at 13,000 years old – appear to be the finger flutings (fingers drawn across soft clay to make patterns) of children as young as two years old. As such, they may represent the earliest known record of creative acts by children.

It should not come as a surprise to learn that our distant ancestors showed such creative abilities. Indeed, it could be argued that the success of humans is largely due to a series of imaginative breakthroughs that enabled us to set ourselves apart from our primate relatives and thrive. Those breakthroughs began with the fashioning of sophisticated tools from stone and wood, and later saw the development of language and agricultural systems.

We believe that creativity can be considered the *hallmark* of the human race, and its influence continues to affect our lives on a day-to-day basis. Those of us residing in economically more developed countries still benefit from the financial legacy of the industrial pioneers of the eighteenth century, who found new ways to achieve a revolution in manufacturing processes that resulted in the creation of vast wealth. And the everyday lives of most people on the planet in the twenty-first century are touched by another revolution – one driven by innovators in digital technology.

Furthermore, creativity has huge importance at the *individual* level too, including for teachers and pupils. The ability to be creative enables teachers to design inspirational learning experiences that help pupils to reach their potential. For their part, pupils need to be taught to build on their natural creativity – still expressed in their early years through their own modern finger paintings – in order to find new ways to express themselves, think innovatively and solve problems. Creativity is surely the ultimate lifelong learning skill that will help young people to enjoy happy, fulfilling and productive lives, sure in the knowledge that they have a robust problem-solving toolkit that can be applied to any challenges they encounter.

Defining creativity

One of the barriers for teachers in embracing the concept of creativity has been the sense of mystery surrounding the subject in the popular educational literature. This has been fuelled partly by the frequently stated myths around creativity that have clouded the understanding of the concept (see section entitled 'Clearing the mindscape for creativity' below).

In Chapter 1, Steve Padget discusses the various points that need to be borne in mind when working towards a robust definition of creativity, informed by the perspectives of various prominent workers in the field. Our own work on creativity, which was first documented in *The Creative Teaching and Learning Toolkit* (Best and Thomas 2007), sought to bring some clarity to the subject by outlining in the simplest possible terms what creativity means and how it can be developed in teachers and pupils. Building on this work we present in the following box some key definitions and ideas on creativity and related terms.

Understanding creativity

- Creativity is the personal quality that enables people to use their imagination and external stimuli to produce something *new* that has *value*.

- Creativity is expressed initially through *thoughts*, which can be translated into *actions* and which ultimately lead to *outputs*. These outputs (e.g. a painting, work of literature or scientific break-through) and the person who has produced them can themselves be described as *creative*.

- Underpinning creativity is the *creative process*, which individuals follow to generate new ideas (see section entitled 'The process of creativity' below).

The above definitions emphasise the fact that creativity can, of course, apply to *any* area of human endeavour, despite the fact that some disciplines (especially art, dance, music etc.) are traditionally considered 'creative subjects'. As such, examples of creativity in action might include:

- car designers creating ingenious interior features that appeal to customers;
- physicists devising new mathematical models for understanding the universe;
- athletes finding new ways to gain a competitive edge.

The implications of the cross-curricular relevance of creativity for teachers and young people in schools are profound, and require all teachers to consider how they embrace creativity in its various manifestations. More specifically, there are three distinctive forms of creativity that need to be considered:

- *Creative teaching* – where teachers use new pedagogical approaches in an attempt to engage pupils (e.g. using Twitter feeds to track the development of a news story).

- *Creative learning* – where pupils use techniques that lead to creative outputs (e.g. writing a short story that outlines their views on a major social issue of the day).

- *Teaching for creativity* – where teachers provide pupils with tools and techniques to enable them to enhance their personal creativity (e.g. using a pack of cards with different objects drawn on them to spark creative ideas).

Creativity and 'mindbergs'

Icebergs form when pieces of freshwater glacial ice break off and fall into the sea. In popular mythology they display only one fifth of their ice above the water line, giving us the phrase 'the tip of the iceberg', although in reality the amount of ice beneath the waves varies from 50 to 99 per cent. An iceberg is defined as such if it protrudes more than five metres above the sea surface; the curious technical term for a piece of ice that protrudes between five and one metres above sea-level is a 'bergy bit', with even smaller pieces referred to as 'growlers'. All these floating ice blocks represent a real hazard to shipping. There are icebergs in the sea and there are icebergs in our minds too (see Figure 3.1).

The Mindberg Model (Thomas 2010) suggests that there are two domains of thinking – the *conscious* and the *unconscious*. For most of us, the conscious

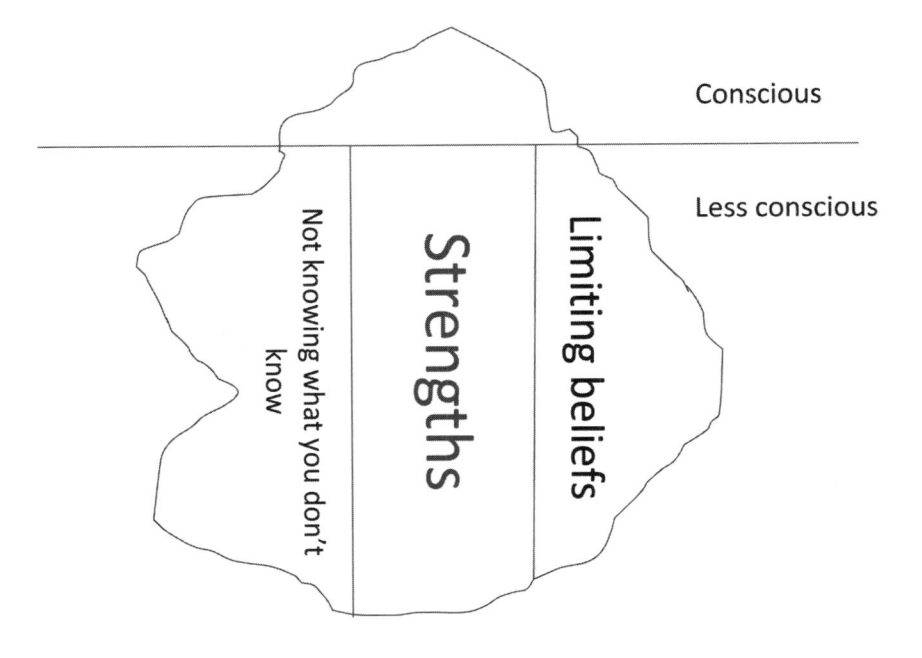

Figure 3.1 Mindbergs in practice

'above-the-surface' processing has a high degree of awareness associated with it. Our self-talk and mental imagery are conscious and therefore accessible. However, beneath the surface – in varying degrees of visibility – are unconscious 'goings-on'. There is a kind of automation about the processing that goes on beneath the water, which makes it difficult to access and which is more intuitive. The Mindberg Model suggests that there are three sub-parts to our unconscious thinking:

- *Not knowing what we don't know* – the ignorance of knowledge, skills and attitudes that may assist the execution of tasks and relationships.

- *Our strengths* – that which we are capable of and which is comfortable and affirming to us, including knowledge, skills and attributes.

- *Limiting beliefs* – ideas we no longer question, which become prisons to us and stop us from thinking and acting differently.

The conditions for creativity

The unconscious thinking domain of the Mindberg Model is highly relevant to the development of creativity, and touches upon creative teaching, creative learning and teaching for creativity. In Best and Thomas (2007) we suggested that, in order to prosper, creative processes require certain conditions (see Figure 3.2). These conditions rely heavily on the development of awareness of the unconscious level of thinking.

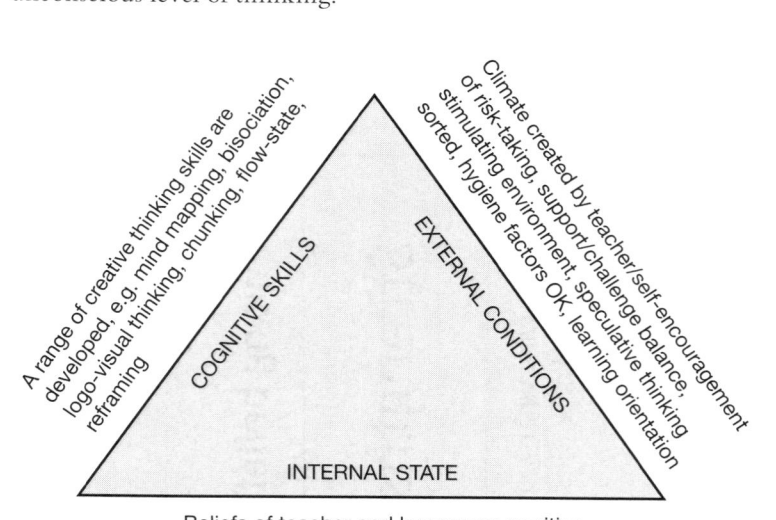

Figure 3.2 The conditions for creativity

Source: Reprinted from Best and Thomas (2007), by kind permission of Continuum International Publishing Group, a Bloomsbury Company

The *internal state* refers to the readiness in the mind of pupils and teachers to be creative, and is associated with the willingness to take risks, try new combinations, allow wild and unusual thoughts to be considered and let go of old patterns and constructs; for example, letting go of beliefs such as 'we have always done it this way', 'there is a right and a wrong way to do things' and 'I am afraid of failure' etc. The appropriate internal state for creativity is characterised by a high level of self-esteem, which comes from teachers recognising and embracing pupils' strengths and the challenging of their beliefs or 'personal constructs' that limit thinking processes. Individuals who can also work as *generative thinkers* (Wilkinson 2006) tend to be more creative in solving problems. A generative thinker is one who is not attached to their ideas in any kind of egotistical way. They are focused on generating and using ideas to achieve an end result, rather than hanging on to ideas for their own personal sense of self-aggrandisement.

The *external conditions* relate to the climate within which a teacher or pupil is operating, that is, the prevailing cultural expectations. Environments that favour and encourage experimentation and delight in the unexpected, curiosity, discovery and dreaming are likely to foster greater levels of creativity.

Cognitive skills are the tools that enable people to be creative. Providing experiences for teachers in their professional development, and pupils in classrooms, to actively engage in problem solving, to talk out loud as they think and to use other cognitive strategies encourages the development of analytical, evaluative, associative, bisociative and abstract thinking. These can all play a role in creativity.

In an ideal world, creativity thrives in a climate where positive external factors are abundant, although in reality they are rarely abundant. We suggest that helping young people and teachers to develop a resourceful internal state and the cognitive skills to generate creative thoughts may fortify them against unfavourable external conditions later in their lives. Indeed, some of the most creative outcomes emerge from external hardships, but we would suggest that they always emerge from resourceful internal states and the cognitive flexibility of the creative person.

Clearing the mindscape for creativity

We have already suggested that limiting beliefs can imprison teachers and pupils and prevent creative thinking and outcomes. A 'mindscape' for creativity is a free, fertile, imaginative, unfettered thinking space where all things are possible. Developing an appropriate mindscape for creativity is vital because our beliefs are filters on the world we experience. When we buy a new car and it's blue, we suddenly notice a myriad blue cars on the road when before they were mainly red (in line with our previous car, which was red).

Beliefs are ideas we no longer question. They are flexible, however, and challenging beliefs is no more complex than asking questions. In the mindscape of many people there are some common beliefs or myths that tend to hold them back from creative thinking. Here is a selection of these myths, with some of the useful challenges to them.

- **Myth 1: 'Creativity is effortless and spontaneous'**
  A study of the world's most creative thinkers suggests that while there may be times of great spontaneity (when they are in a state of what has been called 'flow' (Csikszentmihalyi 1991)), there is a process underlying their efforts and being creative also involves considerable effort, determination and focus.

- **Myth 2: 'Some people are creative, others are not'**
  The evidence points to the fact that creativity is learned not hardwired. If we surround ourselves with people who have well-developed creative skills, we are likely to learn how they do it and become more creative ourselves.

- **Myth 3: 'Highly creative people are on the fringes of society, renegades and unemployable'**
  Creativity can be channelled for the purposes of everyday problem-solving as well as really visionary thinking. It can be practical and relevant to a range of mainstream professions in addition to taking us on incredible imaginative journeys.

- **Myth 4: 'Creativity is just an arty thing'**
  Across all walks of life, from science to politics, from economics to religion and from highly innovative forms of modern art to traditional artistic pursuits, creativity can enhance outcomes and bring real, tangible benefits. It may be that creativity has traditionally been associated with mainstream arts due to the ease with which the creative outcomes of the arts can be communicated to others. Mathematicians and scientists, on the other hand, may find it harder to convince people outside their field of their creativity.

- **Myth 5: 'Creativity is a luxury we cannot afford in difficult times'**
  We believe that, due to the current economic, social and environmental challenges our world faces, creativity is a *necessity* we cannot afford to ignore. The skills of creative thinking and thinking skills in general have never been more important in finding the resolutions to the problems faced by the human race. It is, therefore, vital that young people today develop creative skills, enabling them to live productive lives and engage with the issues that they will face.

- **Myth 6: 'Creativity is frivolous and undisciplined'**
  Thomas Edison's work to develop a light bulb hinged on creative thinking. Many of the most creative people in the world now work in the media, developing both new communication platforms and the engaging content that they communicate. There are rules that work in generating creative ideas and cycles and processes that underpin them (see the Creativity Cycle below).

Whether you are operating from an iceberg or are further along your journey and therefore working with 'bergy bits' and 'growlers', we would encourage you to examine your own beliefs and get colleagues and pupils to do the same. We want to stress that creativity should not be seen a peripheral activity in schools, but instead should be considered central to the work of teachers as classroom innovators and influencers of young people. Creativity is also essential to young people themselves, so that they can live successful working and personal lives, and make their contribution to a happier, more just and sustainable lifestyle for all global citizens.

The process of creativity

All major studies of creativity point to the fact that creative ideas are not just the result of generating random thoughts. Instead, it appears that a sophisticated underlying *process* underpins creative thought and problem solving, guided by a clear objective. A significant part of our recent work on creativity has centred on examining this process with the aim of breaking it down into its constituent parts. This is an important step forward, because if an individual is to become more creative, they first need to understand the key elements of the process.

Our research suggests that there are eight stages to the creative process, and we have devised the Creativity Cycle to illustrate these (Best and Thomas 2007; see Figure 3.3). A full explanation of the different stages is given in the following box.

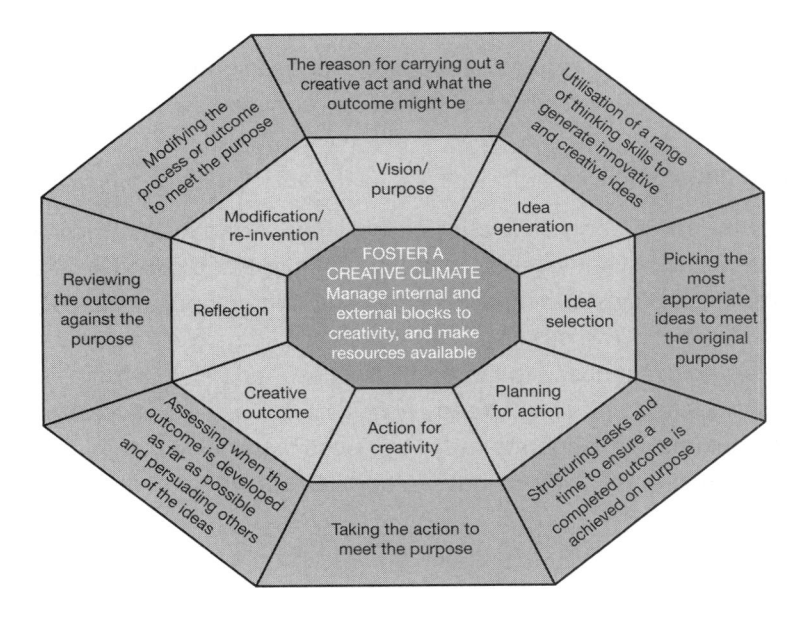

Figure 3.3 The Creativity Cycle

Source: Reprinted from Best and Thomas (2007), by kind permission of Continuum International Publishing Group, a Bloomsbury Company

Stages of the Creativity Cycle

1 Vision or purpose

This stage of the cycle is about clarifying the reason for embarking on the creative process and gets to the heart of the problem to be solved. For a teacher working in a school, potential reasons might include:

- I need to devise a more engaging way to teach about the French Revolution.

- I want to come up with some new ideas to manage the behaviour of a challenging class.

- I need to develop a fresh approach to factual writing.

For a pupil in a school, potential reasons might be:

- I want to write a poem that explains my views on bullying.

- I need to find a new way to present my ideas about the effects of science on our lives.

- I have been asked to consider how my school can reduce its carbon footprint.

This stage can be framed in the context of a vision by considering a point in the future and what will have been achieved by that time.

2 Idea generation

This is the most cognitively challenging stage in the cycle. It involves the use of internal and external stimuli and a range of thinking skills and tools such as brainstorming, bisociation and mind mapping (see Figure 3.4 and Best and Thomas (2007) for more details), in order to generate a wide range of responses to the problem. It is often helpful at this stage to think in terms of having already *achieved* the vision and to imagine what would have changed to make this possible. It is vital at this stage to concentrate on *quantity* of ideas rather than *quality* – that comes next.

3 Idea selection

This stage of the cycle is about selecting the most appropriate idea or ideas from all those generated. To do this it is necessary to revisit

Stage 1 to check the suitability of ideas; it may also be necessary to combine ideas to generate further possibilities. It is also important to establish if the original vision or purpose is still valid. This is because, once we begin to think differently about a problem, the very nature of that problem can shift.

4 Planning for action

This is the stage at which we plan to implement our chosen idea(s) and devise the steps that will allow that to happen. A crucial element of this stage is the order in which the actions will be completed and how much time will be allocated to each one. It is important to prepare a written plan to help move the creative process forward in a timely manner.

5 Action for creativity

This stage involves taking the necessary actions to deliver the creative outcome. These actions could be very diverse in nature but are likely to include work to produce a tangible output that can be seen or heard by other people. In order to achieve a high-quality result it is vital that we show both commitment and determination at this stage.

6 Creative outcome

This is the stage at which, as a result of our actions, one or more outcomes are reached. These need to be judged against the vision as set out in Stage 1 to determine whether or not this has been achieved. It may also be necessary at this stage to convince others of the value of the outcome(s) – to demonstrate how creative our ideas turned out to be in practice.

7 Reflection

This stage requires us to look back over the previous stages of the Creativity Cycle and ask reflective questions to review what has been achieved. These could include the following, which need to be considered through analysis and evaluation:

■ Does the outcome of our creative ideas give us the end result that we sought?

- What has been successful and what is not working?

- What specifically might need to change and what are the limiting factors?

8 Modification or re-invention

The analysis and evaluation carried out in Stage 7 may lead us to the conclusion that the outcome has not fully achieved what was intended. In Stage 8 our initial ideas can be modified or new ideas generated with the aim of achieving a more desirable outcome, this time informed by what has been learnt to date. It will then be necessary to work through the eight steps of the Creativity Cycle once again in order to determine whether the outcome is indeed more desirable.

The numbered stages of the Creativity Cycle suggest that it is necessary to work through the cycle sequentially, beginning at Stage 1. However, we recommend a more flexible interpretation of the model where different entry points are used depending on the context. For example, a teacher could begin at Stage 7 ('Reflection') by evaluating the success of a new teaching strategy introduced by the senior leadership team. In this case the teacher would first make judgements on the success of other people's creative ideas, before addressing the problem themselves by working through all stages of the Creativity Cycle.

Practical tools for creativity

It is important to recognise that some people may be effective when operating at certain stages of the Creativity Cycle, but not others. For example:

- A pupil may be good at selecting the best idea from a list of possibilities (Stage 3), but find it hard to generate a diverse range of ideas to choose from (Stage 2).

- A teacher may be effective at planning for creative action (Stage 4), but find the next stage of actually carrying through the action difficult to achieve.

- A school leader may be highly skilled at using reflection to establish whether desired outcomes have been achieved (Stage 7), but find the other components of the Creativity Cycle more challenging.

Those people who are able to sustain high-quality creative outputs – at home, in school or in the wider world – are likely to be those who are skilled at *every stage* of the Creativity Cycle. Teachers may wish to provide case studies of such creative people to illustrate that an underlying process guides their achievements – a process that pupils themselves can master through targeted effort. It is imperative that teachers seize this opportunity to improve the effectiveness of their pupils at each stage of the cycle with the aid of a range of targeted interventions and practical tools. We have devised one such tool, the Creativity Web (see Figure 3.4), in order to help pupils understand the specific thinking skills required at each stage of the cycle and the strategies that can be used for maximising their work at these stages (Best and Thomas 2008b).

The Creativity Web has three layers:

- the *inner layer*, which shows the eight stages of the Creativity Cycle;

- the *middle layer*, which displays the thinking skills required at each stage of the cycle;

- the *outer layer*, which provides examples of the practical strategies that can be used to optimise work at each stage – these are explained in detail in Best and Thomas (2007, 2008a) and Thomas (2005).

We envisage that the Creativity Web will be used to support pupils' creative thinking within specific subject disciplines as well as across the curriculum and in their lives outside formal education. It is a simple tool that can bring powerful results by helping pupils understand the different components of the creative process and improve their performance at each of the eight stages of the Creativity Cycle.

The Creativity Web is a flexible tool that can be used to explore additional aspects of the creative process. For example, teachers can provide pupils with:

- a copy of the web with the outer two layers of text removed, and ask them to give themselves a score out of ten for how effective they think they are in using the thinking skills and strategies mentioned at each stage;

- a copy of the web with the outer layer of text removed, and ask them to record the strategies they use as they work through the stages;

- a copy of the web at the end of the academic year with all text removed, and ask them to complete from memory as much of the content as possible.

In addition to the benefits for pupils of the Creativity Web, teachers and school leaders can equally benefit from it in a range of ways. For example, the web could be used by teachers to enhance their creativity in planning and delivering outstanding learning experiences and by school leaders in devising and implementing school-wide innovations to enhance educational opportunities for all.

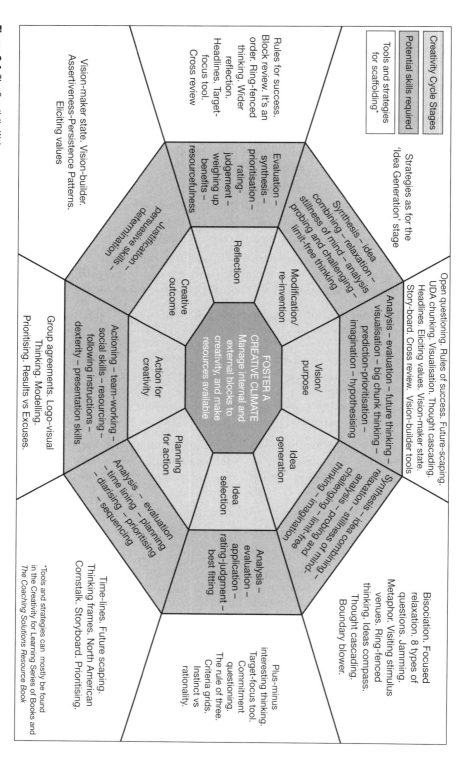

Figure 3.4 The Creativity Web

Source: Best and Thomas 2008b

Teaching and learning implications

The Five Domains of Effective Teaching

In our book *The Creative Teaching and Learning Toolkit* (Best and Thomas 2007), we presented a new way to think about effective classroom practice in a model called the Five Domains of Effective Teaching (see Figure 3.5). The model was favourably reviewed by a range of contemporary thinkers in education and remains, in our view, a valuable tool for teachers in planning, developing and auditing their practice. It outlines six key aspects to effective teaching (with two of these merged into one domain when presented in the model):

- **Vision**
  A vision is an outline of the future, representing the ideal scenario for the pupils in the classroom, department, school, community and so on. It is closely associated with the values of the teacher and the people leading the school.

- **Climate**
  The climate relates to the emotional and physical climate in the classroom. It includes the degree to which pupils are hydrated, oxygenated and working at a comfortable temperature; the classroom also needs to be a stimulating and interactive learning space. Climate also concerns the need for positive, supportive relationships between pupils and their peers and teachers.

- **Teaching and learning strategies**
  A range of teaching strategies should be employed to help pupils reach their potential, including the development of creative thinking skills.

- **Reflection**
  This is the process of teachers reflecting on what worked and what did not work with pupils, and modifying practice accordingly. These reflections can be based purely on personal insight, or through feedback from other teachers, pupils, parents/carers, Ofsted etc. The outcomes feed back into all of the other aspects of the model.

- **Teacher's professional domain**
  It is essential that a teacher knows their subject/curriculum content well, but their possession of up-to-date curriculum knowledge is not enough in its own right. Teachers must be able to do such things as scaffold learning appropriately and plan learning experiences that lead young people to draw meaningful conclusions. These areas belong to teachers' professional competence.

- **Teacher's personal domain**
  For effective and creative teaching and learning to take place, we believe that teachers (and pupils) need to be happy, free from negative stress, fulfilled, healthy, motivated and empowered. Our model differs from many other representations of effective teaching by embracing the *personal domain* of the teacher – a hitherto largely overlooked dimension in the educational literature.

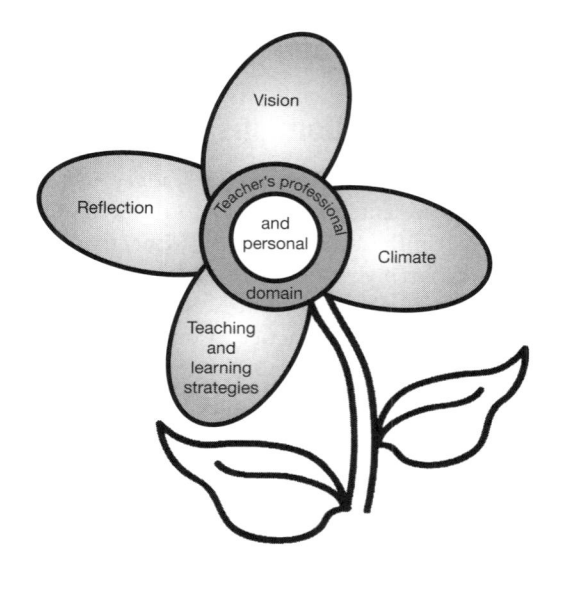

Figure 3.5
The Five Domains of Effective Teaching

Source: Reprinted from Best and Thomas (2007), by kind permission of Continuum International Publishing Group, a Bloomsbury Company

The Creative Teaching Framework

Our research into the importance of creativity in the classroom highlighted the vital role it can play in helping young people to solve problems and reach their potential. For this reason we wanted to make creativity central to our core model for effective teaching. We did this by combining the Five Domains of Effective Teaching with the Creativity Cycle to create a holistic model called the Creative Teaching Framework (see Figure 3.6). This framework puts a creative problem-solving approach at the heart of teaching and learning excellence.

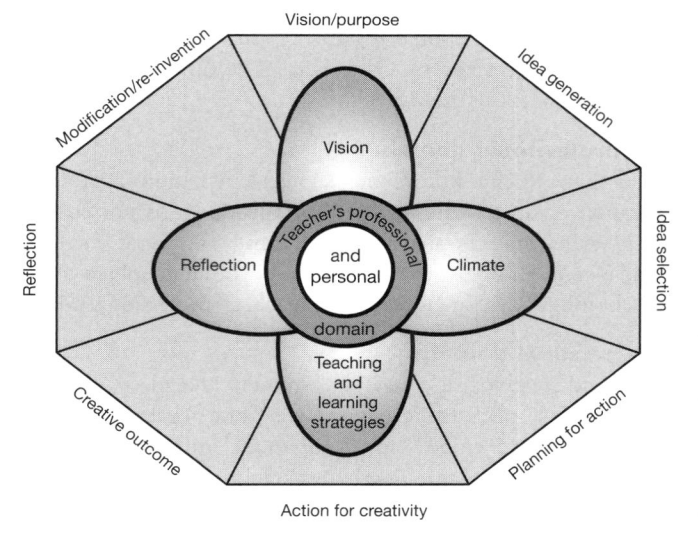

Figure 3.6
The Creative Teaching Framework

Source: Reprinted from Best and Thomas (2007), by kind permission of Continuum International Publishing Group, a Bloomsbury Company

Creativity tools for the classroom

The Creativity Cycle can be used by teachers to generate solutions to a range of challenges that influence teaching and learning, as shown in Table 3.1.

TABLE 3.1 Using the Creativity Cycle

Creativity Cycle stages	Key questions	Responses/ actions
1 Vision or purpose	What are you seeking as a positive outcome in this area? What would you prefer as outcomes (in relation to what is currently not working)? What are the blocks to these outcomes and how might they be lifted?	To be completed by the teacher
2 Idea generation	If you didn't have to worry about the blocks to this vision what might you do? What are all the ways you can think of (however wacky, unusual or serious) that might work or trigger further interesting ideas? Consider someone else's viewpoint ... what would they suggest?	
3 Idea selection	What might work? Which of the above ideas could you combine to make the new result even more potent? Check your chosen idea against your original vision/ outcomes: will it do the job? Will it do so with integrity? What is positive, negative or just plain interesting about each idea?	
4 Planning for action	What will you do and when will you do it? What is the critical pathway to success? What would a timeline of key actions and events look like that outlines what needs to happen in order for this idea to work successfully? Who else needs to be involved?	
5 Action for creativity	How would you use every sense (including visual, auditory and kinaesthetic approaches) to communicate your idea and get people using it, working with it or accepting it?	
6 Creative outcome	When you have your outcome check that it measures up to your original intention. Is the outcome fit for purpose?	
7 Reflection	As you reflect on the creative process and outcome, what can be learned?	
8 Modification or re-invention	Is there anything you need to do differently to get the outcome you hoped for? Is there anything that would make the process faster, more effective or more efficient next time around?	

Case study 3.1: Improving teaching and learning

A teacher in the third year of her career at a school in London used the Five Domains of Effective Teaching to carry out a half-termly mini-audit of her progress. She created time in the penultimate week of each half-term to carry out work on the self-evaluation tool based on the model that appears in Best and Thomas (2007), reflecting on her strengths and areas for development in the coming half-term. The Creative Teaching Framework also allowed her to follow a cycle of thinking to generate solutions to issues that arose, without getting too bogged down in them. It also allowed her to objectify her responses more effectively, in much the same way as Table 3.1 does.

Many teachers have become interested in how creative ideas might be *measured* and we have developed a tool called the Creativity Barometer (see Figure 3.7) to enable them to attempt that process (Best and Thomas 2008a).

The Creativity Barometer asks the user to look at their creative outcome and assess the degree to which this is both *new* and has *value*. The barometer can be used by both pupils and teachers – see the case study below.

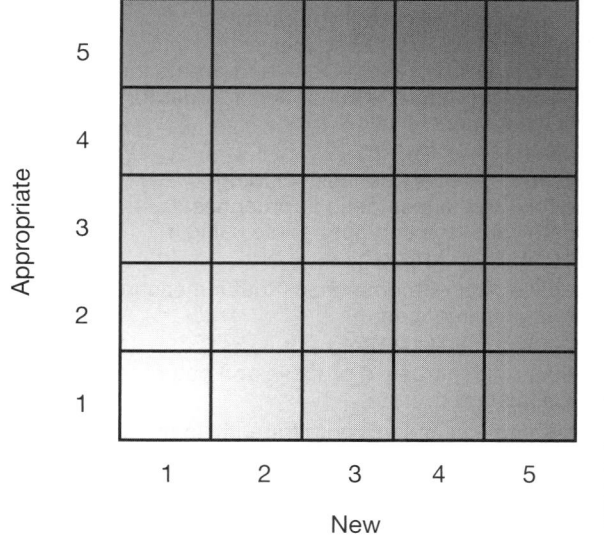

Figure 3.7
The Creativity Barometer

Source: Reprinted from Best and Thomas (2008a), by kind permission of Continuum International Publishing Group, a Bloomsbury Company

Case study 3.2: Working with the Creativity Barometer

A teacher wanted to explore how creative her pupils had been in a lesson on the importance of original experiments in science. At the end of the lesson she handed out copies of the Creativity Barometer to the pupils and explained what the two axes meant. She then put the following question on the board: 'To what extent have I been creative during this lesson?'

Pupils were then challenged to mark a cross on the barometer grid at the point of intersection between two scores, one for the concept of 'novelty' (i.e. they had not had the idea before) and the other for 'value' (i.e. the idea was relevant to the subject of the lesson), where 5 is the highest possible score. The teacher supported the pupils by providing a worked example from a previous lesson of how a pupil might assess their creativity, referring to the twin concepts of newness and value. Furthermore, any pupils who struggled with this activity were given one-to-one support.

The pupils were then asked to reflect on their Creativity Barometer. The nearer the cross was to the top right-hand corner of the grid, the more creative the pupil had been in the lesson. The teacher then encouraged the pupils to consider whether ideas had to be new to have value, as several individuals had crosses at the top of the grid (indicating a high degree of value) but not positioned towards the right-hand side (indicating only a low to moderate degree of novelty).

The teacher concluded that the Creativity Barometer provided a practical tool that enabled pupils to assess how creative they had been in particular learning episodes. It also allowed pupils to explore the relationship between the novelty and value of ideas.

Leading creativity in schools

In writing this chapter we wanted to place creativity at the centre of outstanding teaching and learning, to help provide some context for the chapters that follow. We believe that the purposeful, innovative use of resources, space, language, skills and knowledge allows pupils to be highly motivated and to learn quickly. If teachers can rise to the challenge, they can make schools places of *creativity apprenticeship*, where young people can gain one of the most valuable life skills.

While the development of the appropriate internal resource state and cognitive skills is key, we believe that, within the learning cauldron of a school, getting the external conditions right maximises successful outcomes for teachers and pupils. School leaders must make sure that *all* pupils are given the best chance to develop creative mindscapes and skills through creativity-enabling leadership. The following five principles will help to nurture and grow pupils' creative capacity:

- Staff development activities should demonstrate that creativity is valued and creative thinking is nurtured.
- Leaders should model creative thinking out loud, regularly and publicly.
- Leaders should share the processes by which decisions are arrived at throughout the school, with reference to creativity.
- Leaders and teachers should involve pupils in activities that model, foster and teach creativity.
- Leaders should reinforce a 'No Failure, Only Feedback' culture at every level of the school.

Case study 3.3: Encouraging creativity across a school

A young headteacher of a primary school in Scotland asked his children to devise at least two possible solutions each time they brought a problem to a member of staff. He also asked his staff to do the same, so that pupils could see it happening around the school and learn from it. He also encouraged teachers and non-teaching staff to model problem solving by talking it through out loud at every opportunity in front of pupils.

Extended thinking

- In your experience what are your (a) personal and (b) professional experiences of the myths surrounding creativity?
- As a result of reading this chapter, what has been confirmed and what has been challenged in your concept of creativity in relation to learning and teaching?
- How does your personal relationship with creativity agree with and differ from the Creativity Cycle?
- What implications does this chapter have for the leadership of innovative classroom practice, either within your own classroom or at a strategic level within schools and colleges?

References

Best, B. and Thomas, W. (2007) *The Creative Teaching and Learning Toolkit*, London and New York: Continuum International Publishing.

Best, B. and Thomas, W. (2008a) *The Creative Teaching and Learning Resource Book*, London and New York: Continuum International Publishing.

Best, B. and Thomas, W. (2008b) 'The Creativity Web', *Learning & Teaching Update*, May.

Best, B. and Thomas, W. (in preparation) *The Creative Teaching and Learning Compendium*, London and New York: Continuum International Publishing.

Csikszentmihalyi, M. (1991) *Flow*, New York: Harper Perennial.

Thomas, W. (2005) *The Coaching Solutions Resource Book*, Stafford: Network Educational Press.

Thomas, W. (2010) *Introduction to Coaching Resource Pack*, Worcester: Institute of Educational Coaching Press.

Wilkinson, D. (2006) *The Ambiguity Advantage*, Basingstoke: Palgrave Macmillan.

4

Sowing the seeds

Creativity and critical thinking in a Key Stage 2 setting

Andrea McLoughlin and Carmel Anne Hodson

Key questions

- How can a school capture, nurture and facilitate natural creativity and promote critical thinking?
- Why is it essential that this happens early in the learner's journey?
- How does this begin the development of learning skills that must be continued in KS3 and beyond?

Introduction

This chapter acknowledges that education is a continuum and to understand fully how a learner's natural creativity and critical thinking develop we have to look at the link between what has taken place in the early part of the learning journey and what needs to be continued into Key Stage 3 and beyond. We will illustrate good practice in creative learning and teaching and the nurturing of critical thinking within the primary phase and show the need for the continuity of provision across the phases to be recognised. In the primary phase the focus is fundamentally about developing the skills of the learning process rather than the acquisition of knowledge. Our hope is that readers from training and from KS3 settings will feel more informed about the extent to which the development of creativity and critical thinking has frequently been part of the learners' experiences already, and appreciate that this understanding needs to be reflected in the methodologies of KS3. Creativity and critical thinking underpin the entire curriculum and it is a limited view that confines creativity to subjects such as art, drama and English, and critical thinking to science and mathematics. This has been demonstrated in the work we have undertaken and have outlined later in this chapter.

We are primary teachers working in a school in a socially and economically deprived area where the average attainment on entry to the Foundation Stage is below the nationally expected level. It is from this starting point that we begin our journey into KS2 at the end of which our learners leave with generally average or above average national levels for reading, writing, speaking and listening and mathematics. It is between these two points that their experiences are formed. We view education as a collaborative enterprise undertaken by adults and learners as co-constructors of their learning. We aspire to build the foundations of thinking to provide learners with the intellectual and dispositional tools they will need as they progress into the secondary phase and beyond. We feel that this is a critical time in the development of creative thinking and learning and these skills have to be nurtured as early as possible. 'Today's schools need to be educating not just for exam results but for lifelong learning ... Pupils/students need to have learnt how to be tenacious and resourceful, imaginative and logical, self-disciplined and self-aware, collaborative and inquisitive' (Gornall *et al.* 2005).

John Holt, in *How Children Learn* says, 'The child is curious ... He is experimental ... He is bold ... He can tolerate an extraordinary amount of uncertainty, confusion, ignorance and suspense' (1983: 139). We know that the young learner is not cautious, but a natural risk taker, and it is this state of mind that allows for real learning. Learning is therefore to be encouraged naturally and intrinsically without boundaries and barriers and it is vital that it is stimulated and encouraged rather than refined, over-controlled and over-directed. Creativity and early critical thinking occur naturally in learners from a very young age and we need to sustain this instinctive nature. 'Children even as young as two want not just to learn about but to be a part of our adult world' (Holt 1983: 139). As adults we can often find ourselves de-skilled in what had been completely natural as a very young child and we must recognise that young learners can usefully lack our hesitancy. We must work with young learners to keep them nourished and supported in an environment of opportunity and challenge.

Traditionally the teacher has been seen as the 'sage on the stage' (King 1993), performing, conducting and 'doing' education to the pupils. This transmission model of education can lead to pupils acquiring and rehearsing a limited skill set without developing a true understanding of learning for life. Learning is seen by many, both outside and still sometimes inside educational circles, as an acquisition of knowledge often on a narrow, rather inflexible path, being passive rather than active. This is now considered to be outdated and at risk of leaving our pupils ill-equipped for the age in which they live. A social constructivist approach, characterised by learning that is social, contextual, sensory, multi-layered and motivational, is what we need to achieve (Continuing Education n.d.); here the learner is at the centre of the process.

Constructing knowledge

Our model has been to view the teachers as co-learners, providing wide and rich opportunities where creative and critical thinking can be taught distinctly, and, moreover, explicitly, with the necessary time and environment given to develop and practise learning. From a social constructivist perspective we see learners interacting with each other, using information to manipulate ideas and calling upon their prior knowledge. Alison King refers to this as the student being like a carpenter or sculptor who 'uses new information and prior knowledge and experience ... to build new knowledge structures and rearrange existing knowledge' (1993: 32).

The transmission or didactic model of teaching can inadvertently damage learners' willingness to take risks and openness to making mistakes by being too prescriptive. In this traditional model, learners are given information that they consider to be correct and unalterable. They do not need to think about the facts given to them, just learn them and reproduce them verbatim. This can lead to learners who are unwilling to question, query and think for themselves and ultimately this will create learners who are passive and unquestioning. Natural curiosity and self-initiated learning, whereby mistakes are to be learnt from, are lost. Creativity and critical thinking should be an ever-present unbroken thread through every learner's journey. Best practice would suggest that what happens very early in this journey is vital and needs to be continually developed in order to make a confident, creative and critical thinker. It is the role of the teacher to ensure that this can be achieved and the teacher must understand why and how these developments occur by bringing these concepts into the classroom through:

- providing contexts for learning;
- encouraging collaborative learning;
- allowing opportunities for learners to formulate their own questions;
- supporting learners as they create their own layers of meaning.

(Continuing Education n.d.)

The need to begin this learning journey as early as possible was in fact acknowledged by the Department for Children, Schools and Families (DCSF). Good practitioners have a clear sense of the entire continuum of a learner's experience and particularly recognise the value of the previous stage and their role in providing a foundation for the next. Just as KS3 practitioners acknowledge the contribution of KS2, primary practitioners look back to the Foundation Stage to see what has gone before. The Foundation Stage is a place of exploration, choice, decision making and discovery. The use of a collaborative approach between practitioners and learners is very conducive to the development of early natural curiosity and openness to learning. For teachers in KS3 to recognise the value of the balance between adult-led and learner-initiated activities promoted in the Early Learning Goals and to feel empowered to incorporate a similar degree of flexibility in their own practice would be highly beneficial. As learners travel through to the later stages of education the content has been seen to become more prescribed, and the delivery more didactic and lacking the flexibility of approach that generates creativity and critical thinking (Cockburn 2001). The social constructivist approach not only allows for greater flexibility throughout the continuum but also sustains other elements of the Foundation Stage that are critical to fostering quality, long-lasting experiences for our learners, such as opportunities for greater degrees of autonomy and freedom, opportunities to make choices for themselves and beginning to understand the need to act responsibly in a more sustainable and progressive manner (Cockburn 2001).

School ethos

With these ideas in mind our school has adapted the curriculum to explicitly develop a more creative and critical thinking approach to learning and teaching. Our notion of creative learning comes from the need to say something about what we are aiming to do across the school in terms of the benefit to all learners. It demonstrates our understanding of a value set based on the development of individual potential that emphasises the value of deep and authentic educational experiences (Sefton-Green 2008).

The development of creative thinking skills enables learners to:

- generate ideas;
- suggest possibilities and hypotheses;
- apply imagination;
- experiment and create new connections.

(Fisher n.d.)

By using critical thinking skills learners are able to:

- form concepts;
- develop the ability to reason;
- research and enquire;
- evaluate and make decisions;
- most importantly to question and discuss with others.

(Kislik n.d.)

We see the acquisition of these skills as a fundamental part of the ethos of the school and not simply an 'educational raincoat' to be used when required. So how are these creative and thinking skills put into practice?

From KS2 to KS3

The active introduction of creative approaches is taking place widely across all key stages, fuelled by the need to educate effectively for the twenty-first century. The use of a wide range of creative techniques (see Appendix 1) has been seen to enhance the effectiveness of the delivery of the statutory curriculum in both primary and secondary settings.

Cross-phase initiatives

Creative approaches such as P4C (Philosophy for Children, see Chapter 7) have been used very effectively in cross-phase initiatives that have been shown to have a range of benefits: for teachers, where staff from neighbouring schools across the phases have created opportunities to train, plan and work together, and for learners who benefit from approaches that take them beyond skills development into the development of dispositions at the same time as easing the transfer between phases.

One cross-phase initiative in Sheffield has run for three years. Here the focal point is a large secondary school and the objective of the P4C day held in June is to help the Year 6s from a wide range of feeder primary schools to begin to integrate before taking their places in the much larger school setting later in the year.

This initiative has had benefits for all concerned; members of staff across a wide range of schools have been able to work together and the new intake has a good opportunity to spend some time in the new, larger school. The learners are introduced to P4C in their primary school, some in the early days of KS2, and are able to use these skills in the events of the induction day.

In the 'Great Learner Project', Buckinghamshire teachers combined P4C and SEAL (Social and Emotional Aspects of Learning) in a cross-phase initiative designed to look at the practical aspects of designing learning where spiritual, moral, social and cultural issues provided the essential framework (Moore 2011).

PLTS and SEAL

The growing understanding of the need to adopt creative approaches can be seen in the embedding of PLTS (Personal Learning and

Thinking Skills) and SEAL within the curriculum, thus providing 'joined-up' learning provision. Creative learning and teaching approaches are those that can help to take a view of the whole learner. It is essential that these approaches are maintained throughout the learner's passage through all the school phases, as the development of the characteristics and dispositions of a learner depend on this kind of approach.

Thinking classroom, thinking school

In our curriculum we have woven together many aspects of creative and critical thinking and the methodologies that are needed to develop and promote thinking in the classroom; examples of this in practice are two projects recently undertaken. The opportunity to put this principle into practice arrived when we became involved with Curious Minds. This is an organisation whose remit was to deliver the Creative Partnerships programme. The programme brought creative workers such as artists, architects and scientists into schools to work with teachers to inspire young people and help them learn. It was introduced in response to *All Our Futures* (NACCCE 1999), which recommended new priorities in education. These included a much deeper emphasis on creative and cultural education and also a balance between learning knowledge and skills in the curriculum and having the freedom to innovate and experiment. In this context we have drawn on a wide range of expertise, including utilising external agents such as Curious Minds to facilitate the process of equipping our learners with the tools necessary for becoming innovative, productive and resourceful adults. In using these agencies we were able to demonstrate in the real school setting how thinking methodologies can be developed and promoted for the benefit of learners by the use of novel, challenging and authentic learning experiences.

Planning the projects

The key approach is to help learners to increasingly understand themselves as being active in their learning through their growing comprehension of cognitive and metacognitive techniques. The plans for the projects 'Keeping Warm' and 'Bad Word' were first discussed in class with learners' written thoughts recorded and displayed in the school publicly for all to respond. So from the very outset the learners were involved in the planning process through Pupil Voice. Initially the whole of Year 4 were asked how they like to learn and how they learn best. This was achieved very simply by asking the children as a year group about their preferred learning styles. The feedback showed that learners were most engaged and motivated when the learning style involved exploration and investigation in practical and thought-provoking situations.

The Foundation Stage model of teaching, of which child-led learning is the vital component, was considered to be a key element to the project's future success. In the Early Years environment, learning is irresistible. Far from following a transmission model of education, learners are facilitated to lead and construct their own learning. It was this model that was adopted for the 'Keeping Warm' project.

Pupil Voice – a matter of entitlement

The issue of Pupil Voice, listening effectively to what learners say and being prepared to act upon it, raises serious questions within a school. Issues of identity, of involvement, of relationships and of trust among those who teach, learn and work together have to be thought about and the implications understood. Bragg (2007) says that 'pupil voice undoubtedly troubles existing relationships and identities, but it also fosters new ones'. Wider and deeper measures of understanding are created between the members of a school when the potential of Pupil Voice is realised.

Pupil Voice is, along with Learning to Learn and Assessment for Learning, one of the components of 'deep learning' described by Hargreaves (2006), one of the core features of personalised learning, and an essential part of the forward movement of child-centred approaches to learning and teaching (Jackson 2006). In taking a stance that elicits and then listens to Pupil Voice we are examining what schools do under six key ethical and professional headings:

- *Educational values* – an assertion that the students are people who matter in schools.

- *Community values* – posing the question: whose school is it?

- *Rights* – an assertion of the fact that students are a significant voice in schools.

- *Social responsibilities* – an understanding that young people have rights and responsibilities now enshrined in international law.

- *Legitimacy* – that there is an authenticity of student perspectives about learning and school community.

- *Pragmatics* – an understanding that if students are not allowed to change what they do, then we will never transform learning.

(adapted from Jackson 2006)

In the secondary phases Pupil Voice is most frequently seen in the context of School Councils. It is estimated that 80 per cent of primary, secondary and special schools have a functioning School Council (Whitty and Wisby 2007) and there are those schools who have pupil representatives on the senior management team and on appointment panels.

In schools where Pupil Voice is heard effectively the logical extension is to involve learners in the co-construction of their learning – the design and implementation of lessons and schemes of learning. In such schools the dynamic has changed and the concept of Pupil Voice has moved from being a forum for the expression of learners' preferences to a culture of partnership with teachers in learning as well as all the other aspects of school life.

Pupil Voice – practical issues

- *Staff training and ethos*: After initial whole-school staff training covering how to listen to, record and use Pupil Voice effectively within year groups and across the school, the staff were able to develop a unified approach. The practice is now embedded into the school ethos; learners understand what they can say and that their opinions are listened to and valued.

- *Cameras*: A range of methods of gathering opinion are used across the age range. Some learners use cameras to photograph the things in the school that they like and those that they do not like. These photographs provide the focus for class discussion and are shared with all staff.

'Keeping Warm'

The objective of this work was to build sustainable staff confidence in areas of the curriculum not usually considered as giving scope to creativity. One of the key outcomes was to acknowledge the role of parents as co-learners and to illustrate the limitless nature of learning. The field of learning for the first project was science. Called 'Keeping Warm', it was a social constructivist approach that was adopted with the creative agent facilitating a series of challenges and problems.

Our aims were to:

- explore a variety of ways in which plants, animals and humans keep warm;

- work creatively in the teaching and learning of the topic of keeping warm;

- harness the power of parental involvement in learning from the very beginning;

- develop the ideas used in the 'Keeping Warm' project into other areas of teaching and learning;

- examine the impact of teaching and learning in 'Keeping Warm';

- celebrate success with members of the wider school community.

Family Workshops

As well as listening to learners we made clear recognition of the role of parents as partners in education. Always included in the Early Years, yet often forgotten as the education bandwagon moves on into KS2, parents are the missing link for many of our learners. The engagement of the learners and the arousal of their curiosity were achieved by asking them together with their families three simple questions:

- What would you like to learn about during the 'Keeping Warm' project?

- How would you like to learn about keeping warm – what kinds of activities would you like to do?

- How would you like to present your work to each other, your teachers and your families?

Families came together in afternoon workshops to discuss the questions, where a flexible approach promoted the inclusion and participation of as many parents as possible.

- One group session looked at learning preferences through picture stimulus cards ranking their learning styles.

- Another group recorded, on large rolls of paper, everything they already knew about the topic of keeping warm and questions or ideas they would like to explore further.

- The last group explored ways they like to remember their learning.

Cleverly, these ideas were gathered on a 'washing line' (merely a rope and some pegs) with each idea written on to a garment-shaped piece of paper and then attached to the 'washing line' to be displayed, acknowledged and read by all. Far from this being seen as a knowledge-gathering topic or transmission of science facts, the learners were asking the questions and in many cases providing the answers. How do plants, animals and humans keep warm in cold environments?

How is an igloo built? How do people in cold climates survive? How do penguins keep their eggs warm? How does our blood keep us warm? Can we improve our circulation? All these were noted down. The buzz and wow created by these Family Workshop sessions was a catalyst for future planning and learning.

Curiosity was heightened when invitations to the launch day were sent out on paper snowflake templates – when returned these formed part of the 'winter wonderland' display. Curious learners asked questions about snowflakes, their unique shape and size and how they are formed. Receiving the snowflakes was exciting, a clear acknowledgement that parents were engaged in the learning as well.

On the launch day everyone had the opportunity to engage in creative explorations by:

- huddling like penguins frozen on the Antarctic ice;

- dancing and remembering that even in the cold a plant can grow;

- gluing feathers to their hands with lard and submerging their hands in cold water to test for warmth and waterproofing;

- creating a 'winter wonderland' in class complete with 3-D penguins of many species;

- imagining and drawing a super-animal to combat the cold;

- building a walk-in 3-D igloo from hexagonal and pentagonal pieces which could then be explored.

The igloo – cut-out corrugated cardboard pieces held together with large bull-dog clips – was to become an interactive learning tool. Each panel of the igloo had a design on both sides. Some showed an aspect of keeping warm using words, while others had drawings and labelled illustrations showing understanding of the theme. This created a three-dimensional sculpture that could be explored externally and internally. Learners from other year groups climbed inside the igloo with torches to light their way. The igloo was a completely different way to present and transform the learners' hard work. It created a buzz of excitement that permeated the school. Creativity was at the forefront of all these activities, but above all the learning was memorable, stimulating and irresistible and this was recognised by the parents.

One of the final challenges was for Year 4 to design an outfit to keep a paper doll warm. The creative expert presented a paper doll in a Victorian 'cut out and clothe' style. This stage of the project was the culmination of the creative processes and critical thinking the learners had undertaken during the Family Workshops and the Launch Day. Earlier in the project Year 4 had considered the various ways in which penguins have adapted to their hostile environment. They had tested different materials for their wind-, water- and heat-proof properties, ingenious ideas being acceptable and embraced. The idea came up for a bodysuit warmed entirely by hot chocolate and an equally imaginative suggestion was a vest made of bird feathers. Groups worked on the design of the outfits, creating what they had designed through collage on to their paper doll and modifying ideas collaboratively. A further extension of this creative learning activity was to extend the idea to a 'Parent and Child' club. This time parents were invited to learn with their child about how to keep warm using different materials with which they created outfits. Some outfits were then modelled by the learners and others were collaged on to a large cut-out paper doll.

'Thinking Hats'

Interventions were made by the creative practitioner using Edward de Bono's 'Thinking Hats' (de Bono 2000). The 'Thinking Hat' technique has the value of allowing the learner to categorise thoughts and think in one way at a time. The hats also depersonalise the learners' ideas and, rather than it being the learner expressing an opinion or thought, the hat speaks for them (see box below). This technique works well with learners of all ages and is particularly suited to problem solving and planning.

Using 'black hat thinking', which makes learners think critically and analytically about difficulties and potential problems, the learners had to pose and then examine 'what if' questions. 'What if the weather changes and the wearer of the outfit needs to cool down?' was a question asked by one group. On their design brief the learners then allowed for these modifications, thinking back to how the Antarctic penguins cool themselves down by fluffing out their feathers to release trapped warm air. Another solution arrived at for cooling down was to have hot water that was travelling through thin tubes around the outfit cooled down by an ice pack within the suit.

The final stage was to film each group discussing their completed outfit as they analysed the processes that had been developed through the use of the 'Thinking Hats'. The film provided a learning resource that could be used again for the future and shared with parents at a celebration event to mark the end of the project. Having been involved in the project from the very outset, parents were keen to see the final outcome and celebrate the success of this way of learning and could not resist the invitations, this time sealed in silver envelopes.

'Thinking Hats'

The idea behind the Six Hats is for learners to place on their heads invisible coloured hats to help train their thinking – it works equally well with real hats or with badges.

Thinking is broken down into small chunks or segments. Everyone thinks in the 'same direction' or wearing the same hat at the same time. The hats have the added benefit of depersonalising learners' opinions.

The Six Hats are a great tool for helping learners to think for themselves.

White Hat	What information do we need?
	This hat helps the learner separate fact and fiction. The White Hat can be thought of as blank piece of paper ready to be filled with everything the learner knows about the issue.
Red Hat	How do I feel about this idea?
	The red hat allows thinkers to explore emotions without justifications. Expect to hear statements such as 'I don't feel comfortable with that idea', or 'what a great suggestion.'
Yellow Hat	What is good about this idea?
	This is the hat of optimistic thinking. While wearing this hat the learner can think of benefits and advantages of an idea.
Black Hat	What are the drawbacks?
	Not to be thought of as a hat of negativity, rather a learner can analyse potential risks and pitfalls. This hat can often complement the yellow hat.
Green Hat	What is possible without limitations?
	The hat of creativity. Unlike blue-sky thinking, this hat allows the wearer to stay in the perceptual stage, without the need to evaluate ideas, thus allowing all possibilities to be exhausted.
Blue Hat	What thinking hats are needed?
	Learners consider the bigger picture while wearing this hat. This is the hat of thinking about thinking, or metacognition. Wearing this hat a group might reach a conclusion. This hat could also be worn to decide on the order of hats to wear when thinking about an issue.

The hats can be worn in any order and no more than one hat should be used at a time. Not all the hats have to be utilised and this might depend on the age of the learners. Hats can be introduced one at a time until learners are confident about what type of thinking each hat requires. The hats are cross-curricular and purposeful in many situations. The hats can be adapted to suit a teacher's individual requirements, making them an essential component in the creative and critical thinking practitioner's classroom.

(Source: www.teachingexpertise.com, *Gifted and Talented update*, issue 62, March 2009)

Benefits and outcomes

'Keeping Warm' had the value of reaching and engaging with parents, teachers and learners from the very beginning.

- Learners had taken on a spirit of enquiry and asked scientific questions; they had had space to solve problems creatively and a tool, the hats, which helped that process.

- By communicating with the parents about the learning as an ongoing process, the outcomes for learners in terms of motivation, questioning, creativity and confidence were made clear. Parental contributions were sought and fully appreciated.

- Practitioners could see that science can be taught by using creative approaches and felt more self-assured about this way of teaching and learning, confident that it could be transferred across all areas of the curriculum.

'Bad Word'

In the 'Bad Word' project we made a film using a digital audio-visual approach to encourage our community of learners to reflect critically on effective communication. The project examined how our words and behaviours affect others and took most of a year to complete. It involved two whole-year groups and resulted in the successful production of a powerful film featuring members of the Year 3 and Year 6 groups. The completed film then became a resource for use across the school.

This was a major undertaking and arched across key areas of the curriculum: ICT, literacy, numeracy, drama, PSHE and citizenship. 'Keeping Warm' had developed our understanding of the importance of parents as co-learners and investors in learning and it had also provided us with new strategies to achieve this effectively. In 'Bad Word' we aimed to continue the development of this involvement and extend it to the wider community.

We reflected on the African proverb 'It takes a whole village to raise a child' because it is vital to acknowledge the influence of the whole environment on learners' development in order to fully understand their needs. The *Every Child Matters* agenda sought to take account of all areas of a child's life through the five aims of good health, personal safety, enjoyment and achievement, making a positive contribution and achieving economic well-being. By drawing on the wider expertise of those around us such as parents, community members and external professionals, we have a much greater ability to meet these aims and inject vital creativity into our learning and to present diverse examples and experiences of critical thinking. If we don't take the 'whole child' into consideration, we miss these valuable, irretrievable opportunities to address life experiences that are relevant to our learners.

The film was produced in partnership with a professional company accessed through our involvement with Curious Minds. Learners' critical thinking was engaged and developed from the start and in the production of the film we focused on:

- *Concept development*: The development of the production was undertaken by teachers and pupils working together. Teachers, learners and members of the school's local community took on the starring roles and were involved with the development of the storyline and character profiles.

- *Research and enquiry*: Learners were responsible for canvassing the views of their local community about the various issues of communication, feelings and emotions that we intended to explore in the film's content.

- *Questioning and discussion*: The research formed a basis for invaluable dialogue between the teachers and learners. It prompted discussion between colleagues and also between the learners themselves.

This was wonderful fuel for a wide range of work undertaken by the learners in literacy and PSHE. It raised the standard of emotional maturity and empathy in a practical way that had an immediate social impact. This was evidenced as the learners became more independent when resolving disputes between themselves and often more patient with each other and more ready to acknowledge each other's needs and differences in a positive and supportive manner. These are essential life skills, enabling learners to be positive contributors to society, and yet the creative nature of the project allowed these developments to happen more naturally and organically, making the learning much more sustainable. This experience impacted positively on other areas of the curriculum as learners were seen to be more open to taking risks in numeracy or science. Rather than being overwhelmed by the wide range of strategies available to them to support learning in these areas, the learners were open and welcoming of these choices. The experience made them more adept and effective in dealing with greater amounts of information. Having a more heightened state of self-awareness allowed the learners to become better judges of, and more confident in, their own ability and so more able to understand their own individual learning needs.

Much of the success of this project was grounded in the way in which it drew on the learners' own experiences of life and took account of what they already had to offer. The material related directly to our community and so was highly relevant to the learners. Learners need to feel ownership in their learning, 'to be in control of their own learning' (Holt 1983) and allowing the learners to take on such responsible roles helped them to invest their energy with enthusiasm and motivation. This sense of ownership was maintained throughout the project and led to some further excellent thinking opportunities.

- **Evaluation and decision making**
  Staff and pupils worked together to edit and develop the final presentation. There were lots of critical decisions to be made and learners had to debate various options related to the editing process.

- **Solution development and leadership**
  Learners from two phase groups were involved. This provided the opportunity for the learners to become facilitators as well as learners. Working with learners from across the age range allowed them to take on new roles and encouraged learners to view a problem from a new perspective.

Sharing learning is as much a part of the process of education as is the acquisition of learning. Learners were able to disseminate their learning through the celebration event held to promote the final edited version of the film to the rest of the school and its immediate community.

The event itself became powerful evidence of the mature learning that had taken place as the learners displayed high levels of confidence and achievement – and just a bit of excitement. To this was added the wonderful feedback from our audience. From the dancing performers to the artists whose work was displayed, and from the speakers to those taking on the role of ushers and hosts, they were seen as confident, expressive, open, sincere, imaginative and mature. Both Year 3 and Year 6 learners took home a sense of achievement and pride. This led to an increase in self-belief and confidence transferable to other areas of their education and lives. Having members of the local community in the audience as well as parents allowed the achievements of learners and teachers alike to be fully appreciated.

Impact

Learners were able to witness first-hand the effect their efforts could have on others, especially their parents, and they were able to see how what they did in school linked with 'real life' This is particularly important for Year 6 as they are on the cusp of transfer. Approaches such as this are particularly effective at ensuring that a learner's creativity and critical thinking develop more fluidity along the continuum. For all of our learners involved this approach helps to sustain their belief in the education system and prevent them from falling into the disillusionment with education that can often be experienced in later key stages.

Reflection

A project such as this does have an official start and end point; however, the valuable lessons remain and can help inform the continued delivery of a creative, critical thinking curriculum.

- The film will be used as a resource in its simplest form. All classes will be able to watch it and use it during PSHE. However, it can also be used as an inspirational springboard for further literacy work.

- Both the staff and the learners of all ages increased their bank of ICT skills. We are more confident using a wide range of equipment and specialist software and will be able to continue to use these skills in new and innovative ways.

- Staff became more highly skilled in different methods of delivery. We not only learnt from working alongside the external partners but we became much braver at handing over control to our learners. The experience has further instilled confidence in the 'guide on the side' methodology and helped us to understand how to be even more effective when we are ourselves learner teachers instead of just being the 'sage' and 'teaching' them.

■   We have a stronger sense of pride, achievement and confidence in our school community. This experience has left all learners involved feeling more encouraged and motivated to continue as active and experimental learners who do not see the classroom walls as a boundary. Education should feel like this to everyone. We all want to have learners who will continue to carry this message. It should be exciting and accessible to all.

Into KS3 and beyond

This chapter has detailed a number of approaches that have proved to be effective in the primary setting and it should be noted that they are equally effective in the later key stages. Because these and other creative methods are generic, they can be stretched and moulded to fit different ages and different abilities of learners, and they work well across the range of subjects in the curriculum. As the current movement, guided by a considerable body of research (see Chapter 1), is now towards an understanding of the necessity to change the way we design and deliver learning opportunities, there is a need for teachers to deepen their own knowledge, confidence and competence in these approaches.

The tool box approach to creative methods could be adopted. Particular methods are more appropriate to certain learning situations, the 'Thinking Hats' technique is very good for problem solving and planning, for example; P4C is good for developing critical thinking and so on. The aim should be to acquire a repertoire of approaches so that each one can be called upon appropriately in its turn. The underlying principle in all of these approaches is the presentation of learning opportunities that are collaborative and language-rich and will contribute to the development of learning skills as well as learning itself.

Discussion points

■   What creative approaches have your Year 7 learners experienced in their primary schools?

■   What do you need to do in order to support and develop these effectively?

■   What creative approaches are appropriate for use in your subject area?

■   How are the learners' voices heard in your school?

Useful websites/resources

www.buildinglearningpower.co.uk/what_it_is.html Guy Claxton's *Building Learning Power* website.

www.curiousminds.org.uk Curious Minds

www.earlyyearsmatters.co.uk/wp content/uploads/2011/03/eyfs_learn_dev_creativity(1).pdf EYFS *Creativity and Critical Thinking*.

www.thirteen.org/edonline/concept2class/constructivism/index_sub2.html Concept to Classroom web page about constructivism in the classroom.

References

Bragg, S. (2007) '"But I listen to children anyway" – teacher perspectives on pupil voice', *Educational Action Research*, 15(4): 505–18.

Cockburn, A. (ed.) (2001) *Teaching Children 3 to 11: A student's guide*, London: Paul Chapman.

Continuing Education (no date) *Constructivism Learning Theory*. Available online at www.lifecircles-inc.com/Learningtheories/constructivism/constructivism.html (accessed 17 October 2011).

de Bono, E. (2000) *Six Thinking Hats*, London: Penguin.

Fisher, R. (no date) *Tools for Thinking: Helping pupils take greater responsibility for their own learning.* © The Highland Council/Robert Fisher. Available online at www.hvlc.org.uk/ace/aifl/docs/highlandmodel/toolsforthinking.pdf (accessed 9 November 2011).

Gornall, S., Chambers, M. and Claxton, G. (2005) *Building Learning Power in Action*, Bristol: TLO.

Hargreaves, D.H. (2006) *A New Shape for Schooling?* London: Specialist Schools and Academies Trust.

Holt, J. (1983) *How Children Learn*. Available online at www.arvindguptatoys.com/arvindgupta/hcl.pdf (accessed 27 July 2012).

Jackson, D. (2006) *Why Pupil Voice?* Available online at www.ncsl.org.uk (accessed 27 March 2012).

King, A. (1993) 'From sage on the stage to guide on the side', *College Teaching*, 41(1): 30–5.

Kislik, R. (no date) *Thinking Skills Vocabulary and Definitions*, Adprima. Available online at www.adprima.com/thinkskl.htm (accessed 15 August 2011).

Moore, W. (2011) 'Developing great learning', *Teaching Expertise*. Available online at www.teachingexpertise.com/articles/developing-great-learning-11767 (accessed 14 June 2012).

National Advisory Committee on Creative and Cultural Education (NACCCE) (1999) *All Our Futures: Creativity, culture and education* (The Robinson Report), London: HMSO.

Sefton-Green, J. (2008) 'Introduction: What is "Creative Learning"?', in Sefton-Green, J. (ed.) *Creative Learning*, London: Creative Partnerships, Arts Council England, pp. 7–14.

Whitty, G. and Wisby, E. (2007) *Real Decision Making? School councils in action*, Research Report DCSF RR001, London: Institute of Education.

5

A question of integration

Creativity and critical thinking in the context of MTL accreditation

Kirsty Coomber

Key questions

- If we teach creatively do learners gain a richer understanding of their own learning?
- What impact does the learning environment have on teaching and learning?
- What impact can the study of creative approaches to learning have on classroom practice?

Introduction

Teachers in training are required to absorb much valuable educational theory, but as they take up their first posts they frequently become submerged in a system that measures their success through the academic achievement of the learners in their charge, the focus being on the results of education rather than the process of learning. Many newly qualified teachers therefore feel under pressure to adopt a transmission approach to teaching, believing that this is how best to contribute to the school's academic targets. There clearly exists a conflict between theory and daily practice. Factors such as the lack of time to plan and discuss strategies with colleagues, coupled with departmental pressure to ensure that targets are met, mean that creative teaching and learning opportunities risk becoming buried. The pressure from established departmental orthodoxies and pedagogies is inexorable, leaving the theory to remain just that. In this chapter I will show how a reading of the work of Claxton on learning dispositions and the importance of the learning environment, of Best and Thomas on creative teaching and learning, and of Alexander and others on the importance of language in learning have influenced the pedagogy of two recently qualified geography teachers.

This was a project undertaken by two recently qualified teachers as part of the Master's in Teaching and Learning (MTL) programme. The aim was to examine the impact of creative teaching and dialogic learning in an environment richly stimulating of language and learning – a potentiating environment. This work was designed to contribute to the coverage of the MTL objectives: teaching and learning; assessment for learning; and how children learn and develop. There was also some coverage of the curriculum development and subject knowledge for teaching objectives. The impact of the work was assessed from the point of view of the value to the teachers of the co-planning and co-delivering of major learning episodes based on creative teaching and learning principles, as well as the value to learners of this methodology. The influence of the success of the work on departmental colleagues' perceptions of how creative teaching methods can be used in the geography classroom was also taken into account.

Behind the practice

The research-based development of our understanding of the social constructivist view of learning has given us a useful perspective from which to view the learning and teaching processes, and we can examine the limitations of the traditional behaviourist approaches that until recently have been the norm in many schools. It is clear that there needs to be an understanding of powerful twin motivations that exist in learners. On the one hand there are performance goals (knowing, looking smart and looking certain), and on the other hand there are learning goals (gaining mastery, gaining skills and applying effort). When the practice in the classroom, influenced by a target-setting culture, promotes performance goals at the expense of learning goals, the effect is to squeeze creativity and enquiry out and learners become concerned with their ability level to the exclusion of all else. A culture of caution is generated where intrinsic motivation is undermined and learners are defensive and debilitated in the face of obstacles. The result is that the personal creativity and the capacities needed to approach cognitive tasks are left undeveloped (Dweck 1986).

The creative classroom is the place within a learning community where learning goals are in an appropriate association with performance goals, where the skills needed to develop the processes of learning are promoted and where the level of intrinsic motivation is high. This places a great deal of responsibility upon the teacher as the significant variable in the creation of the learning environment because higher learner achievement has been seen to come from the successful creation of a 'thoughtful and learning centred climate' (Watkins 2010: 6).

Creativity in its simplest form is the process of finding and implementing new and appropriate ways of doing things (Best and Thomas 2007), and is expressed through actions and outcomes that themselves are seen as creative. Claxton (2006) looks at the variables under the control of the teacher which, when balanced, can produce a climate in which creative learners thrive. These include:

- the use of time;
- the use of space and the visual environment;
- the activities offered, encouraged and allowed;
- the materials and resources available;
- formal and informal assessment;
- the language that is used to comment on learners' actions, achievements and products;
- essentially, consideration of that part of the learning environment that will help to promote the value of, and utilise, learners' uses of language.

The influence of an understanding of these factors on the design of creative learning is profound; their effective incorporation into learning design promotes and nourishes creativity in both teachers and learners.

Four learning environments have been identified that have the power to restrict or promote the creativity of learning and teaching (Claxton and Carr 2004) and the features of these are detailed below. The successful creation of a potentiating environment was a developmental target for this project. By creating the right environment the development of learning dispositions could be planned for. Gornall *et al.* (2005: 5) list the four 'learning-power' dispositions as:

- *Resilience* – the emotional aspects of learning.
- *Resourcefulness* – the cognitive aspects of learning.
- *Reflectiveness* – the strategic aspects of learning.
- *Reciprocity* – the social aspects of leaning.

The prohibiting environment

The first environment identified by Claxton and Carr (2004) is the prohibiting environment. Here 'a tight schedule results in the learners moving rapidly from one activity to the next, prohibiting pupil collaboration' (Claxton and Carr 2004: 5). One could make associations here with the restrictive timetables of many schools alongside the traditional expectation that the teacher's role is to impart knowledge. The resultant environment is repressed, learners are not afforded the opportunity to engage with a topic over any period of time, the teachers transmit the body of required knowledge to the empty vessels within a structured short period of time and learners are expected to be compliant, the passive supporters of the teacher's purpose. Under this regime little time is given to developing learning dispositions, and opportunities for learner talk and collaboration are strictly limited, if present at all, and there is no recognition of the individual learner's needs in respect of learning style. No opportunity is given for learners to question, digest or discuss the subject matter and the teacher has no means of gauging engagement and comprehension other than the expressions on the mass of faces in the class.

The affording environment

The second, the affording environment, allows learners to develop learning dispositions but, as this is incidental and not planned, the activities for learning do not move the learners forward in a dynamic way. In this environment there is the tacit assumption that the appropriate dispositions do not need to be *taught* as they will be *caught*. One could liken this to the relationship that many schools have with the personal learning and thinking skills (PLTS) agenda of 2007. Secondary teachers are aware of the skills and competences contained in curricular guidance, and identified within schemes of work; however, the lack of explicit teaching of these attitudes in some schools means that there is no scope for learner development. Many teachers did not adapt their teaching to facilitate the required challenge and needful growth so the creative opportunities were in many cases missed. An example of the affording environment can be seen in the traditional 'tutorial' style lesson. Learners passively listen to the teacher's delivery; they are compliant and support the teacher's purpose in that. There may be an opportunity for the learners to develop resourcefulness as they are given the opportunity to discover links with previous subject matter, and they may be able to increase their reciprocity as they listen to each other and discuss the questions arising, but these dispositions will not be developed unless they are made explicit as part of the learning of the lesson.

The inviting environment

The third, the inviting environment, values questioning and actively encourages working collaboratively. Here the teacher has changed the pedagogy as new and appropriate ways of doing things are implemented (Best and Thomas 2007). No longer is the teacher merely attempting to transmit knowledge, but is providing opportunities for active learning to take place. In this classroom there is time to unpick the learning and, through the regular exercise of skills, the learners become more resilient, more resourceful, more reflective and able to form better relationships. Such teaching leads to greater retention and improved cognitive and social progress by learners, the key being their move towards ownership and active participation in the learning process.

Many outstanding teachers subscribe to this model, recognising the value that comes from the conscious engagement of the learners. Within such lessons one would see enthused learners participating in challenging tasks resourced to facilitate independent learning. The opportunity for active learning improves the social skills of the learners while providing valuable opportunities to assess the learning and intervene when necessary.

While this environment fosters creativity and initially looks to provide the optimum learning environment, it also provides constraint as the teacher is still solely responsible for directing the learning throughout the given time frame. The learner establishes meaning and exercises the dispositions, however the learning trajectory for the lesson is set and rarely negotiated. The learning objectives and predicted outcomes are shared at the start of the lesson and the learners' understanding of the concept is established through an enquiry guided by the teacher. At the end of the lesson the learners have worked socially to establish meaning and will have exercised a number of learning dispositions – they have grasped the concept; however, the natural quest for learning is curbed by the need to meet the directed objectives and outcomes for the lesson. There can be little deviation from the set objectives as the straitjacket of time and the prescribed curriculum determine the final outcome. This significant drawback, the lack of negotiation and flexibility, is addressed as a dominant feature of the fourth environment.

The potentiating environment

The fourth environment is referred to by Claxton and Carr (2004) as the most powerful environment, yet this in my experience is the one that is the most difficult to set up, manage and maintain. It involves a significant amount of risk taking and skill but yields significant rewards for teachers and learners alike. Within the potentiating environment challenging questioning is used to stretch the learners' collaboration and is recognised as an essential skill, but the critical difference is the relationship that exists between the teacher and the learners, as here power is shared. This environment has the potential to generate creative thinking and both the learner and the teacher are deeply involved in the learning process. Within this environment the role of the teacher is principally to facilitate and support learning and enquiry. The learning experience generated in this way is richer as the learners are actively engaged in the learning process and have some control over its nature and direction (Rogers and Freiberg 1994); there is the potential for co-construction of learning. For this to take place the learners have to communicate and establish meaning and connection through dialogue with their peers. It is here where the concept of assessment for learning is fully deployed and has a striking impact as the talk within the lesson not only engages the learner but also informs the teacher about how the learning is progressing and what needs to be done to accelerate and consolidate it (Alexander 2008). At a different level the design of learning in this way acknowledges the role of language in the development not only of learner skill, knowledge and understanding, but also of learner identity.

While this environment is the ideal, providing the optimum experience, it takes skill, time, patience and courage to establish. The status quo is being questioned and the demands of resources, time and location made by the deployment of interactive and creative methodologies must be addressed minutely in the planning because they could show significant differences from the norm. The successful creation of the potentiating learning environment must be the goal of every teacher as they journey through the profession, because of what it says about their understanding of learning and the needs of learners and their role in that process.

The challenge of the project

The challenge for the teachers was clear. They were to develop their pedagogic skills in the production of a series of learning episodes designed explicitly to foster learning skills. They were to encourage deep engagement and the ability to solve problems together, make decisions and develop resourcefulness. Rather than teaching concepts the teachers were challenged to create an environment where learners were stimulated to create meaning through dialogue as they devised solutions to a range of problems. The learners' findings and their solutions would be presented collectively at the conclusion of the lesson sequence. This called for challenging collaborative strategies demanding of intense participation, shared responsibility and significant engagement. It meant that the teachers needed to step back, observe, fulfil a different role than they usually did and be prepared to experiment and then reflect. In short they were to be creative, finding novel and appropriate ways of doing things, thus leading to creative actions and outcomes.

Planning for learning

Establishing a potentiating environment is no easy feat. It was therefore imperative at the outset that time was given for planning, discussion, consultation and experiment, a luxury often not available within the daily constraints of the working day. The teachers began to think about the what, when and how, addressing the issues of time, resources and methodologies as well as the learning objectives, the curricular objectives and the formal and informal assessments that would be made.

The need for the daily restrictions of school organisation and timetable were recognised and where possible lifted, and resources were made available through the use of the staff and facilities of a City Learning Centre. Quality time was set aside to examine the learning process and create strategies and develop activities that would provide a rich learning experience. The school's hour-long timetabled session did not provide time for learners to 'get stuck' and 'work it out'; it was therefore decided to deliver the learning in two sessions, each of 210 minutes. When planning each session there was a concern that the learners may struggle to concentrate for such a sustained period of time; however, it was clear after the first session that the more time they were given to immerse themselves in the learning the less aware of time they became.

The learning sequence consisted of two extended and thematically related episodes three weeks apart (see box below). Concepts relating to important environmental issues were to be discussed. Learners' voices were to be heard as they moved towards formulating answers to the key questions and throughout the sessions the emphasis was to be on language used together to make meaning.

The learning sequence

Session 1: What is the environment?

The groups examined their concepts of some of the main environmental types in the world and then began to look at the impact of the use of fossil fuels on the environment with specific reference to global warming.

Session 2: Why are alternative energy sources important?

The information and experience gathered from the first session was deepened as the groups were tasked with producing a news broadcast arguing for the use of alternative forms of energy generation.

The use of rich resources

The teachers wanted the learners' enthusiasm and creative output to be fuelled not only by the learning activities but by the ignition of the learners' senses – by a physical environment that immediately grabbed the imagination of the learners as soon as they entered the room. The vision was to use ICT as a tool to transform the learning experience rather than provide a mechanism to capture it. Stimulating resources were found including artefacts, film and still visual stimuli designed to provide the starting points for group tasks, posing questions that would demand collaboration and discussion as conclusions were arrived at.

On entering the room a sense of 'awe and wonder' was created as the learners were plunged into the subject through the use of 4-D design software. The work space was different and there was an instant awareness that this was a 'different lesson'. The room layout provided opportunities to work collaboratively; the large room had areas that could be screened thus offering flexible spaces; desks were set out in groups but not in a conventional manner and there was room to move around; it was easy to hear the discussions of the nearby groups and feed from their ideas and enthusiasm. Tablet computers with internet access were available for each learner and these all worked without any technical hitches (something that rarely happens within the real classroom), allowing learners to engage in the research as needed with a strong element of self-direction.

Activities for rich learning

During the planning process the teachers were aware that they needed to provide a learning journey in which the learners could establish meaning and definition through enquiry and discussion. Opportunities had to be created where dialogue provoked challenge and disagreement as well as consensus (Lindfors 1999), alongside those fostering joint enquiry where the learners were able to construct shared meanings from different stimuli that ambassadors brought back to the common learning task (Barnes and Todd 1995).

Tables 5.1 and 5.2 give an overview of the activities for learning and the resources used over the two sessions. From the outset the learners were in groups of four or five and broadly remained in these groups throughout the sequence. The objectives were ambitious and the resources were plentiful and this included an advantageous staff ratio with a lead teacher, two teachers in support and the services of a technician.

TABLE 5.1 The range of creative learning activities related to resources – Session 1

What is the environment?

Cognitive objectives: To achieve an understanding of the term environment. To achieve an understanding of the importance of the environment. To be able to explain how we get electricity from fossil fuels. To have an understanding of the impact of getting energy from fossil fuels.	*Learning objectives:* Working together in a group. Listening to others in the group. Making contributions to the group work. Analysing and sorting information. Making decisions together
Resources LogoVisual Thinking Board: Key question: What is the environment? Visual stimuli: Ambassadors visit exhibits and relay information to the group. Rally Robin (Kagan technique): What do humans need to survive?	*Activities:* Sharing initial understanding of the term and beginning to arrive at an agreed definition. Concrete evidence to help to conceptualise characteristic features of different environments. How does this information help to modify the agreed definition? Learners iterating and sharing information in a structured and cooperative way.

Magnetic white wall: Key words.	Looking at key words and discussing how they can be categorised – placing words on magnetic wall – collaborative exercise to assist decision making and discussion.
Video presentation: The overuse of the environment – before and after photographs.	Stimulation of response and discussion. Use of deep questioning by teacher to seed discussion – development of peer–peer and learner–teacher dialogue.
Surprise box – collection of related items.	Create sequence of items – stimulation of discussion to develop understanding of how coal is turned into electricity. Decision making.
Interactive questions using signs, floor mats and opinion stations.	Promoting expression of opinion, dialogue between peers and opportunity for disagreement and discussion.

TABLE 5.2 The range of creative learning activities related to resources – Session 2

Why are alternative energy sources important?

Cognitive objectives: Investigating the advantages and disadvantages of a specific energy type. To be able to explain the advantages and disadvantages of this method. To be able to make informed decisions about the impact of this source of energy on the lives of people and the environment.	*Learning objectives:* As Session 1 plus: Developing research skills. Collaborating creatively. Evaluating own work. Evaluating the work of others. Learning to explain these judgements.
Resources iPad computers 1:1	*Activities:* Guided internet research – access, selection and evaluation skills – note-making task to support information gathering and recording.
Simulation using ICT/video: The island is about to run out of energy – how are you going to avert disaster?	Discussion and manipulation of information to solve problem – deciding on suitable alternative source of power.
Top Secret information pack: Visual and written information to seed discussion and provide key questions.	Evaluation of information against a range of criteria and decision making.
Video camera and green screen: News broadcast.	Preparation of oral presentation to be performed to camera as news item. Use of previous experience and information to synthesise – to create and perform the news item to camera. Learners evaluate own performance and that of other groups against specific explicit criteria.

Facilitation rather than transmission

The teachers were guided by the need to facilitate rather than transmit as they created a series of activities that would allow learners to establish meaning through physical prompts, research and collaboration. However, doubts were raised at times in the minds of the teachers and significant questions were asked about the value and importance of the underlying principles of the project. The balance between teaching subject knowledge and fostering learning skills was questioned, debated and at times unresolved. It is easy to see why many teachers lapse into the apparent safe mode of transmission in a system that assesses performance of their learners in a limited period of time. Time spent fostering, exercising and mastering the skills associated with learning should be seen as an investment that will help to accelerate the acquisition of subject content and better contextual understanding. It is essential that these two aspects of learning go hand in hand. The teaching technique that has to be mastered could be called, in Claxton's phrase, 'split screen teaching', where the content curriculum and the learning curriculum are planned for and taught explicitly side by side. This is the infusion principle and it is described by Carol McGuinness (2000) in the ACTS (Activating Children's Thinking Skills) research; this key research into thinking and learning is described in Chapter 1.

In order for infusion to work McGuinness says that teachers need to be supported in:

- recognising the need to be explicit about the processes of thinking and learning as well as the content;
- the development of their own understanding of a range of thinking skills;
- their ability to readily identify contexts or topics within the curriculum that can be matched with particular thinking skills;
- the development of planning and teaching that meets both high-quality thinking skills and curricular content objectives; and
- the development of a vocabulary for talking about thinking that is suitable for the age and ability levels of the children in their classroom.

Formal and informal assessment

While the learners' dispositions would be developed within the learning processes the school measures attainment by written means, predominantly under exam conditions, and focuses on knowledge acquisition and the interpretation of this. It was necessary, therefore, to consider this to ensure the learners' preparedness for the written element that would follow the experiential sessions. The key components of the written task were addressed in the preparation of the oral presentation. The final written assignment was to take place under test conditions at a future date and this would be assessed against National Curriculum attainment levels. Data from this and a previous cohort were compared – had the learning experience proved to be richer and more effective?

The development of the learning dispositions (using Claxton's definitions) would be informally measured through teacher observation and more formally by asking the learners to comment on how they felt about the success of their learning. The teachers were looking at the learners' ability to be:

- *Resilient*: Based on their knowledge of the learners the teachers were able to assess concentration and perseverance and compare it with their experiences with other groups and these groups under regular classroom conditions.

- *Resourceful*: By observing the level of pupils' questioning that took place and seeing how well the learners were able to make links and establish meaning.

- *Reciprocal*: By observing the learners' enhanced ability to cooperate and collaborate, thereby demonstrating the value of the social aspect of the learning.

- *Reflective*: Observations were made of how well the members of the groups had been able to unpick the learning and reflect on the process.

Impact on learners

At the end of the first session it was apparent that the imaginative approaches taken had motivated and stretched the learners. Learners reflected that they really enjoyed the session and felt they had learnt more as it was fun and interactive. Meaning had been established through experiential learning rather than by the transmission of the teachers' knowledge and the learners felt that they had been actively involved in the learning process (Rogers and Freiberg 1994). Questions had been used to clarify meaning and they had left this session with knowledge about, and an enthusiasm for, the topic. Learner enjoyment and engagement was evident throughout the lesson as they worked industriously for significant periods of time.

Undoubtedly the vision, environment and learning strategies used had produced engaged learners who were prepared to look for solutions to problems and call upon their resourcefulness to do this. Evaluations were made of the effectiveness of the methodology and these thoughts fed into the planning of the next session. The frequent opportunities for learners to engage in decision making deepened their understanding and also provided the foundation and point of departure for the following session. Good dialogic teaching challenges not only children's understanding but also our own, demanding a secure conceptual map of a learner's subject matter (Alexander 2008). The early misgivings of the teachers had gone and the conversation during the planning of the second session had changed focus from content to learning.

The project was an opportunity to approach things in a novel way so, for the second session, a fictional scenario was created, placing the learners within a 'live' situation through the use of the available ICT resources – the groups were on an island with a restricted power source; they had a set time in which to make decisions about planning realistic alternative sources of energy based on responses to the contents of the 'top secret' information pack. Technology facilitated the illusion and somewhat unexpectedly amused the learners. A significant period of time was allowed to pose questions, identify problems and issues and so the opportunity was there for debate and discussion of their thinking (Alexander 2008).

Working closely together in the time available the learners were to conduct an investigation into the advantages and disadvantages of a range of possible energy sources and report their findings publicly to the rest of the group in the form of a live news broadcast. Here was the stimulus of an imaginative topic. Moving from the concept of the wider environment the learners were beginning to tackle some of the issues connected with the impact of the use of fossil fuels in power generation and how they compared with other sources of energy. Here was an opportunity to assess the understanding of concepts through content, oral presentation skills and collaboration skills. The learners were given the performance criteria as they worked on their group presentations so that they were aware of how the piece was going to be assessed. This helped as a guiding framework for the task itself and also for the peer-assessment process that was carried out after each performance. Significant time was allocated to this multi-faceted and demanding task, something with which the teachers were now more comfortable having witnessed the level of concentration generated in the first session.

Measures of success

The project's success was measured through a formal piece of writing. It was pleasing to see that the learners who completed the assignment met or exceeded their expected target grades. Their writing showed in-depth knowledge of the subject, explaining the geographical concepts couched in subject-specific vocabulary. They demonstrated their ability to argue points both for and against each power source. However, the 'hard data' shows only one side of the true learning experience.

Through observation and further questioning the learning experience could be analysed. When asked to reflect on the experience the vast majority of the learners acknowledged that the lessons were interesting, fun and challenging. The learners stated that:

- they enjoyed being able to 'work it out' for themselves rather than being directly taught;
- they found the visual stimuli at times amusing and engaging and the final task challenging, believing they were producing something rather than just writing about knowledge;

- they appreciated the extended time given and enjoyed talking through activities rather than having information delivered that they had to interpret;
- they valued significantly the opportunity of working in a non-traditional environment that was rich in ICT.

All but one of the learners felt they had been challenged, stretched and motivated. That learner (who normally is passive in lessons) stated that he didn't enjoy the lesson as he had to get involved; however, his final attainment level was in line with his predicted grade and showed that he had benefited from this experience. The accessibility of reliable ICT made the research and production feel more real. The teachers were initially wary of this, believing that the iPads and green screen technology could have been distracting. However, the learners used these to facilitate their learning without question. Their facility with, and acceptance of, these tools reflects the technologically rich society within which they operate and served as a reminder that at times we do not fully utilise these powerful learning resources.

These sessions had enabled the learners to experience the exercising of their social language skills in order to approach answers to questions. For the video presentation they had to collaborate, think critically and evaluatively and establish meaning within a group, and also be able to communicate those ideas and conclusions. The dynamic within the classroom captivated the learners as they made focused responses to the wide range of stimuli. Questions raised within the groups were generally answered within the groups and the teachers were consulted in order to clarify meaning. Learners worked industriously towards a common goal with little or no guidance. This climate was created and maintained through the use of a creative approach to teaching, which in turn fostered creative thinking in the learners (Craft 2005). One could surmise that the teachers had fulfilled Hargreaves' (2004) statement in that 'the pedagogy should at its best be about what teachers do that not only helps learners learn but actively strengthens their capacity to learn'.

Reflections

From the findings so far it is clear that the creative nature of the teaching had a positive impact on the learners' motivation and engagement; however, what we must consider now is the impact on the teachers and their subsequent pedagogy. Claxton (2006) states that for culture change to occur the practitioner needs to change what regularly happens in the classroom in order to invite creative thinking and stretch and strengthen creative habits and dispositions. This issue was clearly addressed in this project but the question still remains – would this work have any long-term effect on the day-to-day pedagogy of these young teachers? Did the theoretical knowledge gained from reading the literature significantly impact on the daily practice and, further, would this be a sustainable change? Both the teachers were aware of the school's focus on teaching transferable skills and regularly addressed this within their teaching. They were both 'good' teachers with a passion to succeed. The master's programme initiated a process that demanded a reassessment of their current pedagogical range. By trying something significantly different they were able to extend their repertoire of classroom approaches.

The focus on classroom action research and the presence of a coach funded through the MTL project required them to question the what, the how, the when and the why. This in turn led them to look at literature that challenged their own pedagogy. Through this practical experience the teachers changed how they plan for learning. They are now more aware of dialogic principles in promoting a richer use of learning language and have a better understanding of how to increase participation in the learning process using social constructivist ideas. Although the time constraints and departmental performance pressures have not diminished, awareness was stirred within both teachers of the significance of allowing learners to construct their own meaning through collaboration. Therefore, it could be argued that collaborative analytical work on classroom practice in the early years of a teacher's development is essential. In this way the development of reflective, outward-looking practitioners is supported, enabling them to be aware of the need to underpin their practice with sound research-based theoretical principles. Both teachers acknowledged the value of the learning process that they had been through and found the experience formative as it changed how they approached learning and would be likely to influence day-to-day practice.

The following understandings are of particular practical interest to all who wish to increase the level of creativity in their teaching.

Imagination

- The value to the learners of using creative teaching approaches and the practical implications that arise from this.
- What the key components of creative learning and teaching are and how they interrelate.
- The conception, planning and construction of both the learning path and the learning environment.
- The depth and detail of planning needed if such approaches are to be successful.

Language

- Underpinning creative learning is the creative use of language by the teacher and the opportunities given to use language creatively by the learners. A teacher's understanding of the primacy of language as tangible evidence of both learning and the process of learning is therefore essential. It is this understanding that will inform the learning approaches.

- The value of the dialogic use of language needs to be understood and the nature of its power in establishing deeper meaning and articulating perspectives. It is through language that we think and so to seed deeper thinking we need language-based approaches that will do that.

Empathy

- Where learners are being supported into learning creatively and independently the teacher's role becomes more complex as the learning dynamic shifts.
- The facilitator of learning will understand that there is now a need for a greater degree of democracy and there are areas of negotiation and co-construction.

Time, space, equipment and flexibility

- Time and space need to be used flexibly and this implies the need to have the opportunity to move away from the restrictions of the normal school timetable and, occasionally, the normal classroom.
- The imaginative use of ICT to inspire and facilitate research.

See Chapter 7 for summaries of some of the key creative learning methodologies and notice the commonality across these – the creation of collaborative working groups and the promotion of the use of language within those groups. An examination of these approaches will help to put into practical perspective the points made above.

The value of thinking differently

It would be easy to speculate that the creative approach was driven by the physical environment, rich in available ICT, and markedly different from the usual classroom and with a greater flexibility of opportunity. But on evaluation it was apparent that much of the learning took place because of the structured support given to the learners' construction of meaning through dialogue. A more democratic learner–teacher relationship was created that was different from the regular classroom. The challenge had been to think differently and deliver a lesson in a new way and this had produced a completely new learning experience for both learners and teachers.

This chapter has looked at the developing methodologies and growing skills of two recently qualified teachers. They were given the time, the opportunity and the impetus to look at teaching in a different way and to examine their existing pedagogies. Significant questions were raised by this experience about assumptions made in the organisation and management of learning and teaching. These issues need to be addressed by all teachers irrespective of their breadth and depth of experience if effective creative methodologies are to be developed in schools where the creation of a potentiating learning environment is a school-wide aspiration.

Discussion points

■ How can the organisation of the school day respond to the need for flexibility of space and time for creative learning?

■ How can a culture of enquiry and research be developed to challenge established pedagogies?

■ How can a school foster a collaborative planning ethos?

■ How can the power of ICT be harnessed in the service of interactive, imaginative and creative learning and teaching?

References

Alexander, R. (2008) *Towards Dialogic Teaching* (4th edn), York: Dialogos.

Barnes, D. and Todd, F. (1995) *Communication and Learning Revisited*, London: Heinemann.

Best, B. and Thomas, W. (2007) *The Creative Teaching and Learning Toolkit*, London: Continuum.

Claxton, G. (2006) 'Cultivating creative mentalities: a framework for education', *Thinking Skills and Creativity*, 1: 57–61.

Claxton, G. and Carr, M. (2004) 'A framework for teaching and learning: the dynamics of disposition', *Early Years*, 24(1): 87–97.

Craft, A. (2005) *Creativity in Schools: Tensions and dilemmas*, Oxford: Routledge.

Dweck, C. (1986) 'Motivational processes in transfer of learning', *American Psychologist*, 41(10): 1040–8.

Gornall, S., Chambers, M. and Claxton, G. (2005) *Building Learning Power in Action*, Bristol: TLO.

Hargreaves, D.H. (2004) *Learning for Life: The foundation of lifelong learning*, Bristol: The Policy Press.

Jeffrey, R. and Craft, A. (2008) *Teaching Creatively and Teaching for Creativity: Distinctions and relationships*, Milton Keynes: Open University.

Lindfors, J.W. (1994) *Children's Inquiry: Using language to make sense of the world*, New York: Teachers College Press.

McGuinness, C. (2000) 'ACTS: a methodology for teaching thinking across the curriculum', *Teaching Thinking*, 2: 1–12.

Rogers, C.R and Freiberg, H.J. (1994) *Freedom to Learn* (3rd edn), Harlow: Prentice Hall.

Watkins, C. (2010) 'Learning performance and improvement', *INSI Research Matters*, 34(Summer).

6

New faces in new places

How the arts centre can impact on creative learning

Rebecca Fearon

Key questions

- What does an organisation like the Bluecoat have to offer young learners?

- What are the benefits for learners and teachers working with creative professionals?

- How can teachers in training benefit from contact with creative professionals?

What does an organisation like the Bluecoat have to offer young learners?

The Bluecoat is a hub of creativity in the heart of Liverpool's city centre. Placing a broad programme of contemporary arts and crafts in the oldest building in the city centre immediately brings with it challenges, but also allows for some fascinating juxtapositions of the new and old. Significantly redeveloped in the run up to the city's year as European Capital of Culture, the Bluecoat reopened in March

2008 with vastly improved facilities for sharing its contemporary programme of visual arts, music, live art, dance and literature. With growing visitor numbers of over 600,000 each year, the Bluecoat has faced recent challenges in terms of public funding but has maintained its presence as a creative force for Liverpool.

'The Bluecoat believes that everyone can be creative.' This is the first sentence in the Bluecoat's business plan, placing creativity in a very democratic context right at the forefront of the vision for the organisation. It stands out in this respect from some of its peers in the United Kingdom and beyond. Many arts organisations project themselves as being mainly concerned with sharing the creativity of a few elite individuals rather than with a more general belief in and support of creativity. It is creativity at all levels that interests the Bluecoat and the organisation has a genuine commitment to supporting creativity in many different contexts and at different points in people's creative journeys. Very young children are often involved in some of their early creative experiences through the free family programme and outreach activities. Learners at primary level may get their first opportunity to work with an artist or to visit an exhibition at the Bluecoat. At secondary level the experiences provided at the Bluecoat have enabled learners to develop insights into creative careers that support their own decision making. Many university students use the Bluecoat as inspiration for their studies and volunteer in the galleries in order to gain experience. Artists with exceptional talents are often spotted in the formative stages of their careers and are nurtured by our curators towards their first major exhibitions, new commissions or performances. New creative industries are offered space in our building and support towards planning the development of their businesses. More experienced artists who had their first opportunities at the Bluecoat often return to share their work and experiences with our audiences. The Bluecoat truly aims to represent, support and inspire creative endeavour at all levels and stages.

The organisation has a clear vision to place itself at the centre of the city's creative web and has developed a strong role in terms of supporting small and medium-sized creative industries. This is achieved through the provision of subsidised studio, office and retail spaces within the building for a 'creative community' of artists and creative industries and an intention towards promoting 'wholeness'. Wherever possible the different aspects of life at the Bluecoat aim to weave together for the benefit of creative practice. Many of the artists based in the studio spaces have been featured in exhibitions in the galleries at the Bluecoat. A significant proportion of the creative community have at one time or another contributed to the participatory programme that is delivered with schools and communities across the city. The participation programme feeds back into displays and exhibitions in the spaces, which add to the programme.

There are over 30 members of the creative community based in the building, covering a multitude of different creative forms. They include visual artists, printmakers, a jewellery maker, a silversmith, a contemporary dance collective, textile artists, a writer, illustrators, photographers, fashion designers, a theatre company, a vocal agency, a disability arts organisation, an instrument maker and a fashion events business. In addition, the Bluecoat has associations with designers, branding consultants and performers based locally who often use the Bluecoat as a place to meet, entertain clients and network. Some of the creative community members are extremely experienced in delivering participatory programmes. They have worked with schools and communities for many years and have developed a chameleon-like ability to absorb and reflect the language and cultures of different learning settings. They are knowledgeable about the curriculum and have integrated planning processes used by teaching staff into their own practices. They are able to set learning outcomes for their sessions and ensure that these chime with the requirements of the curriculum. They are often experienced in engaging learners who are harder to reach and in dealing with challenging behaviour. When working with teachers they are able to take a lead role in terms of planning and delivery.

While more experienced practitioners are able to take the lead in planning, it is vital that teachers are equally invested in the planning process. While the artist may only be there for a very limited time, the teacher will usually have an extended relationship with the pupils concerned and can input invaluable information into the planning process, with reference to the preferred learning styles represented in the group of learners. Practitioners may have great ideas but the teacher will know the limitations of resources, including space and time, that could adversely affect delivery if the activity is mismatched with the context. If fully involved in the planning processes and related decision making, teachers are better placed to use the experience to inform new approaches to teaching after the practitioner's involvement is complete. The best possible projects are those where teachers and practitioners work closely together in the planning and delivery in order to make the most of every opportunity for engagement. This can work well even with practitioners who have less experience of working within the education sector. The relationship can be well balanced, with clear roles and areas of expertise, and if enough time is in place for planning a genuinely co-led approach can be the result.

A co-led approach to delivery can be beneficial for many reasons. The practitioner can be themselves and not feel that they have to adopt the role of teacher or disciplinarian. This in turn can make them more interesting to the learners who are often attracted to a different approach as well as a different face in the room. The teacher, who will know their learners better than a visiting practitioner, can ensure that an appropriately inclusive approach is taken and can respond if they perceive particular learners experiencing difficulties. It can also represent an opportunity for teachers to work with learners in a very different context where the teacher can be a learner too, which can support the building of more positive dynamics in a teacher–learner relationship. Teachers will often learn something new about their learners through contact with a visiting creative practitioner, as the experience will often bring interests and aptitudes to the fore that may not previously have been obvious. Teachers should aim to make the most of any opportunity to work alongside a creative practitioner in order to get the best for their learners and for their own continuing professional development.

Between them, the practitioners and staff at the Bluecoat and other arts organisations have a wealth of day-to-day experience of applying critical thinking skills. Problem solving is a daily activity, whether in terms of finding a starting point for a new commission, responding to a difficult brief for a leaflet design or working out how to show a particular piece of artwork. The creative retailers need to be highly critical when selecting stock that they think will sell, using a variety of aesthetic and business criteria to make decisions. Curators are constantly responding as artists change their ideas when creating work to be shown in the galleries with a plethora of knock-on effects. Artists working with participants in outreach projects must be able to process information and respond very quickly to keep participants engaged, showing that creative practitioners are constantly making critical decisions throughout the creative process. When some of these experiences can be shared with learners they not only gain an insight into a growing industry that can provide potential careers, but they are also encouraged to attain new levels of applied critical thinking.

Case study 6.1: Creativity in an informal learning context

The Bluecoat has a small but dedicated team of staff who are responsible for the management of a range of participatory activities, including work with schools. Organisationally, this is motivated by a belief that working with schools can be one of the most effective ways to ensure that young people from a range of backgrounds have access to the arts and to high-quality creative experiences. We have also seen evidence that our resources, when used in the right way, can really bring out the best in some learners, often those who may not usually shine academically.

This is true of our work not only with schools but also with our outreach programme, which aims to target those who are most disadvantaged and at risk. In 2011 the focus of our outreach work was on an area of Norris Green where, with our partners at Liverpool Everyman and Playhouse Theatres, we opened The Pad, a space for creative engagement with the young people who hang out by the shops on the Strand. Many of the young people concerned are at high risk of involvement in crime and antisocial behaviour. Most are young men between the ages of 10 and 19. By employing an ex-offender as a Youth Mentor who works alongside creative practitioners, we are engaging these young people in creative endeavours that aim to help them learn new skills, raise their aspirations and widen their sphere of experience. We have already seen small successes in this area of work with some of the young people proudly exhibiting their photographic artwork and animations.

Creative expression can allow these young people, some of whom have been excluded from school, to maintain some element of positive learning in their lives. It allows them time within their chaotic lives to obtain that state of absorption, or 'flow', that we reach when we create. It is also giving some of them the chance to act like children again, when their lifestyles have conditioned them to behave like men from an early age. But most importantly we hope that we can support them to realise that, just as they make creative and critical choices in our sessions, they have choices to make in life and that nothing is wholly predetermined for them even though that is sometimes how it may seem. Initially the choices we encourage the young people to make may seem fairly small and inconsequential – what effect will you use when altering a photograph in Photoshop, or what shot will you choose when making an animation? Gradually we build towards more important decisions – what project would you like to focus on next, or which artist shall we employ to work with you? They earn this increase in empowerment through their investment of time and effort in the projects; those who give more have more input. This emphasis on choice and decision making, the creative process as a metaphor for life, can have resonance within and outside the formal education context.

What are the benefits for learners and teachers working with creative professionals?

As Head of Participation for the Bluecoat my role has often involved working very closely with teaching staff on the planning and delivery of education activities. Some of the activities have been fairly brief experiences lasting just a few hours, while others have been programmes of work lasting months or even years. The experience of working with an education professional has almost always been a stimulating one. Where possible I have always looked for ways that the Bluecoat could support the existing delivery of the curriculum rather than just parachuting in with a one-off activity. Some of the most exciting work has been when a teacher has been able to outline a problem or issue in the classroom and we have looked for ways that it might be 'solved' through an intervention by an artist or practitioner.

Since 2005 the Bluecoat has had involvement with a programme funded through Creative Partnerships. This organisation put the problem-solving approach right at the forefront of our partnerships with two schools. Having been on Creative Partnerships' course for Advanced Skills Creatives, along with colleagues from Liverpool Biennial and Tate Liverpool, we had together reached the conclusion that contemporary art had the potential to be a fantastic resource for inspiring new approaches to teaching and learning across the curriculum. Contemporary art is all about ideas and, therefore, covers a huge range of subject matter with relevance to many different subject areas in formal education. The ways in which ideas are presented by artists often come from unusual standpoints that engage the viewer in different ways, often evoking strong emotions that we believed could support learning. We worked together to devise a methodological framework to test out our theory and each chose a subject area with which to work.

Creative Partnerships

The establishment of Creative Partnerships in 2002, the Blair government's flagship creative learning programme, was the result of recommendations coming from the Robinson Report, *All Our Futures* (NACCCE 1999). Creative Partnerships were established to develop young people's creativity across England. Arts Council England established a Creative Partnerships team in Merseyside in 2003. The team built a solid reputation for the efficient and effective delivery of the Creative Partnerships programme, developing strategic and operational alliances and partnerships with a range of individuals and organisations across the educational, cultural and regeneration sectors. In 2008 Arts Council England transferred the management of Creative Partnerships to Creativity, Culture and Education (CCE) and 25 area delivery organisations (ADOs) are now responsible for delivering the programme across England.

In the first year I worked with two English teachers from different schools. Each was working with Year 8 classes and we decided they would be the focus of our project together. Both teachers were interested in finding new ways of inspiring the development of learners' creative writing skills by introducing some of the devices and structures that support effective narratives with particular reference to character development. After establishing a shared goal, the second stage of our methodology involved a day out visiting contemporary art exhibitions looking for inspiration. We decided to go to Manchester for the day and visited Cornerhouse, the international centre for contemporary visual arts and independent film in Manchester, the Manchester Art Gallery and the Chinese Art Centre.

Both teachers were clearly nervous about this exercise. Neither was particularly comfortable in gallery spaces and it took a lot of reassurance on the journey to Manchester to convince them that contemporary art was not something to be afraid of. Many people worry that they will not be able to find the answer when they view a piece of contemporary art. Clearly most artists will have a particular idea in their head when creating a piece of work and it is interesting to try interpreting the messages to identify what they are trying to communicate. However, it is also the case that many of these messages can only be decoded by people who understand the specific references in the work. Some of these references may be intensely personal and known to but a few in the artist's inner circle. Other references may relate to other pieces of artwork, or to political, religious or social events, which may or may not be known to the viewer. For this reason I always encourage those who are new to contemporary art not to be afraid to take a more personal approach and respond by using their own reference points. The meaning you will glean from the work may be totally different from what I might feel or from that which the artist meant, but this does not make it any less relevant or resonant. We all bring our own memories and associations with us wherever we go and they will affect how we feel and react to many different situations and stimuli. Most people will not find any link at all with one piece of artwork while finding another incredibly relevant to them. This can be an interesting exercise with young people in a gallery space – find something that is relevant to you and explain why. Reassured and with an open mind, we embarked on our visual art journey looking for inspiration.

At the end of the day we talked on the train home and both teachers had been particularly touched by one piece of work we had seen at Cornerhouse. The piece was a 'found' photograph that looked as though it may have been taken in the early twentieth century in a photographic studio. In the background was a Greco-Roman pillar and distant landscape, but the artist had ripped the central figure out of the photograph, leaving a mysterious space that the imagination automatically worked to fill. This idea of removing a character from their setting and using this as the starting point for imaginative character development inspired an eight-lesson scheme of work delivered by the teachers with planning and resource input from the Bluecoat. A series of photographs was sourced and the details of the main characters were removed so only a shadow remained. The teachers were able to use these images to inspire a range of creative writing experiences, all of which the learners approached with enthusiasm. Eventually the characters were reintroduced and the learners were given a range of fantastical landscapes in which to place them. The scheme of work not only produced some imaginative creative writing, but also seemed to particularly inspire some learners who might usually find such exercises more difficult. Using a visual stimulus as a starting point appealed to different learning styles and was found to be very successful for most learners in the class. The concept also involved a high level of imaginative problem solving as the learners looked for visual clues in the background as to who the main character might be, what they looked like, and what was their story.

In the second year of the research project I continued to work with one of the English teachers, but also worked with two science teachers from the other school. Again we used a similar methodology and this time the ideas were overflowing after our gallery visits, especially for the science teachers who went away buzzing with ideas to bring their curriculum alive using contemporary art references. The project was again deemed successful by the teachers involved and all of them felt that they would use galleries as a resource for ideas in future. I was delighted to hear several years later that one of the science teachers had gone on to become a lecturer in an education department at one of the local universities and was undertaking PhD research into how contemporary art could be used as a resource to teach science with particular reference to astronomy.

Evaluating impact

On entering the second year of my partnership with the English teacher we felt compelled to do some more in-depth evaluation of the success of the scheme of work, seeking proof of the success of the methodology. The teacher used a new scheme of work inspired by contemporary art with one class while using more orthodox methods to teach another parallel class as a kind of control group. We looked at their predicted levels for end-of-year tests and then, after the tests, we were pleased to see that more learners in the class with which we had worked had achieved a higher level than predicted. While this success cannot be solely attributed to our methodology, it was felt by the teacher that there was a tangible link between the scheme of work and the higher levels achieved.

The value of learning outside the classroom: the Diploma experience

The work on the English project was inspired by gallery visits but the activity took place in the classroom and was delivered by teachers. While this approach can undoubtedly enrich the curriculum and inspire new approaches to teaching and learning, there is a whole range of other benefits to be gained when the learning takes place outside the classroom. The Bluecoat was privileged to be involved in the early stages of the Diploma in Creative and Media, working on the delivery of the Level 2 Diploma for three fascinating years. At the point at which I became involved, the Diplomas were in the planning stages and a group of teachers from Knowsley were working together to look at the best ways of offering pupils maximum choice and variety when the Diploma started in nine months' time. There was a certain degree of trepidation as the Diplomas represented a totally new way of teaching and required a radical new approach.

When I read the Diploma curriculum I was excited, and was immediately struck by how well the units reflected the real world of creative industries. There was so much scope for live projects that could result in learners' creative products being used in the 'real world' instead of being theoretical exercises undertaken in the safety of the classroom. This increases risk for the learners, teaching staff and for any venue presenting the work, but in terms of learners gaining valuable work experience and feeling a sense of achievement there was much potential. Working alongside a senior teacher from Kirkby Sports College we started to plan the units for the first year, looking at how the resources of the Bluecoat could be used to support delivery. Each unit focused on the development of a creative product and represented a flexible framework that reflected the universal creative process of initial ideas, critical selection, development of an idea to fruition and evaluation of process and product. Fortunately there was a budget for involving creative practitioners, which allowed us to draw on the creative community at the Bluecoat and involve them in delivering aspects of the units. The Bluecoat was also happy to invest in terms of providing free space for a proportion of the sessions as it was felt that this could be a vital part of the success of the programme.

In our three years of co-delivering the Diploma we involved over 20 different practitioners and staff in delivering experiences for learners. Each unit resulted in some kind of presence at the Bluecoat, from performances and exhibitions to publicity campaigns and even a one-day festival. Learners were able to work directly with photographers, textile artists, film-makers, graphic designers, a performance artist, marketing professionals, illustrators, a silversmith, operational staff and a writer. The practitioners often shared their specific skills but there was also an emphasis on sharing experiences. How did the practitioners get where they are now? What had they focused on at school? What courses or work experience had they undertaken to help them on their journey towards being a full-time creative practitioner? How do they decide when a piece of work is finished? Young people were encouraged to question and to learn about all aspects of people's roles.

To underline this learning they not only produced work to share but also learned about risk assessments, marketing, participation programming and other aspects of producing creative events. In the final year of delivery most sessions took place at the Bluecoat because teachers noted that the young people acted differently when they were in this environment and usually rose to the challenge of being treated like young professionals. This influence of place over behaviour and attitude is fascinating but makes total sense. Once the young people became familiar with, and comfortable at, the Bluecoat they took on many of the characteristics of its other inhabitants. They began to see themselves as part of the creative community with whom they had so many experiences. For learners of this age group who need to develop an understanding of the world into which they will soon move this is a vital step.

In terms of the risks associated with presenting work in a public venue, this was managed in different ways with different groups. Our first group were particularly nervous when undertaking the performance at the end of their second unit. They had been working with a live artist who had introduced them to a totally new type of performance with which they formerly had no experience. Their unit culminated in an afternoon of action at the Bluecoat on Valentine's Day. They had devised a series of performances and audience interactions themed around love and when they arrived at the Bluecoat that morning most of them looked terrified. Roger had brought with him a big bag of pink tutus, which he thought the girls in the group might like to wear. At the start of the day none of the group wanted to wear them and they started nervously with their first performance action, a mobile piece around the reception area and garden.

The Bluecoat is fairly busy at Saturday lunchtimes with an audience who are used to coming across the unexpected in our venue. After the group received a positive and interested response to their first performance, confidence started to grow. When a member of the public used their Valentine message wall to propose to his girlfriend excitement peaked, and before long they were all wearing the tutus (including one of the boys) and were buzzing with creative energy. We have found that the risk usually pays off and, as with people working in the creative industries every day, the achievement of acclaim is the sweeter after the anxiety that preludes the sharing of your work. Amplified in the public realm the anxiety may have been more keenly felt, but the delirium of success soon followed. Of course success is not a guaranteed outcome and teachers must be prepared to support learners when things do not go totally according to plan.

How can teachers in training benefit from contact with creative professionals?

As well as working directly with learners on a range of creative programmes, the Bluecoat is also keen to impact on the continuing professional development of teaching staff at different stages of their careers. This has manifested itself in several different programmes, all of which have brought teachers and those in initial teacher training into contact with creative practitioners and the gallery environment. Building on the success of the first Creative Partnerships collaboration, working with English and science teachers, a second programme also centred on using contemporary art as a stimulus for inspirational teaching and learning experiences. With two schools in Liverpool we developed an approach to working with mentors of trainee teachers, encouraging them to try our methodology and support their trainees to do the same. Following this we planned to deliver a session to the trainees themselves, the aim being to introduce the use of contemporary art to inspire teaching in science, PE, history, geography, maths and English.

The programme started really well with a great session at the Turner Prize exhibition at Tate Liverpool with the subject mentors (the Bluecoat was still closed for redevelopment at this point). They were all really experienced teachers and, despite some initial expressions of doubt, they all came away 'converted' with plenty of ideas as to how some of the artists' communication methods could be utilised in the classroom to reinvigorate some of their teaching. We then ran

a similar session for the trainees, which, it soon became clear, was far more prob-
lematic. During the PGCE programme trainees are taking on board so much
in terms of subject knowledge and pedagogical theory that to introduce a fairly
radical and complex concept early in their second placement was, for most, too
big a leap of faith. Mentors could see how the methodology could bring something new to the way they were communicating some ideas to their learners, but
the trainees did not have that experience. A few of them understood the concept
and went on to develop and deliver schemes of work inspired by their gallery
visit, but others went away sceptical and unconvinced. We resolved that any
future work with trainees would need to be more comprehensive and allow more
time for the concepts to sink in alongside their other learning.

The opportunity to try out a more long-term model of working with trainee
teachers came in 2010, when we were approached by Liverpool John Moores
University (LJMU) Education Department to talk about how we might contribute
to one of their PGCE courses for the following year. Staff were aware of the work
we had been doing with the Diploma in Creative and Media and were interested
to look at how we might distil some of the learning into a package for trainees
undertaking the 14–19 specialist pathway for teaching the Diploma in Creative
and Media. The focus was to be on effective working with arts organisations
and creative industries with a particular emphasis on the Diploma, which at the
time of planning was still being offered as a statutory qualification. We designed
a ten-session course, which would take place over a six-month period and where
the outcome would be delivered as part of a core assignment that the trainees
would be undertaking.

As government policy on Diplomas moved there were changes afoot at LJMU
and, with the funding withdrawn for the specialist pathway, the trainees were
moved over on to an Applied Arts pathway instead. However, it was decided that
the course content was still relevant and that, as long as we stressed throughout
that the learning could be applied across all formal learning contexts, we could
proceed pretty much as planned. The course length was reduced to six sessions
but still over the same period and the first session became part of induction.

Most of the course was taught at the Bluecoat and took the trainees through a
process of learning about the resources we could offer, gaining an understanding
of how the units for the Diploma in Creative and Media worked and learning
about how different practitioners could input their skills and experiences into the
learning process. We also looked at project management, hosting skills, health
and safety, roles and responsibilities and how to make the most of any opportunity to work with a practitioner. As a core element of the course the trainees were
given, in small groups, a particular Diploma unit to develop. They were given
opportunities to meet different practitioners and decide which ones they would
want to work with on their unit. They then met further with their chosen practitioners and went through a dummy planning process, which allowed them to
really understand how to negotiate the relationship and how to integrate contact
sessions into a wider teaching plan. At the end of the course they presented
their unit outlines and explained how practitioners would support delivery. The
results were, on the whole, outstanding and the group really thrived on the

opportunities to meet practitioners and discuss ideas with them within a framework that supported some really thoughtful and informed conversations.

The trainees were very fortunate that LJMU was able to make this kind of investment in their training. Most teachers in training will not have this kind of opportunity unless they are placed within a school that works extensively with creative practitioners. Even then they may not get the chance to really analyse the benefits of bringing a new face into the classroom and they may not be witness to best practice in terms of hosting a practitioner. There are so many practical details involved in arranging a visit from a creative practitioner that can make or break the experience for both parties. Teaching staff are so busy and have so many priorities that sometimes the real potential of a visit is not reached because of a lack of advance information, a lack of clarity in the brief for a practitioner or the provision of unsuitable facilities or equipment for sessions. This is where working with an organisation like the Bluecoat can be helpful. Many arts and cultural organisations now have experienced staff who can help with many aspects of planning a project or session with a practitioner. Some have more of a focus on sessions taking place within their own organisations and others, like the Bluecoat, are interested in supporting sessions in school as well. Many organisations will be able to access funding to make projects possible in the first place, so it is always worth having a relationship with your local cultural sector so that your school can be well placed when these opportunities arise.

Why should teachers make the time?

So, why is it worth making time for initiatives of this nature and adding to workload? Why should teachers spend their own time making arrangements with arts organisations or individual practitioners when there is always so much else to be done? While it is impossible to provide a robust evidence base that these interventions work for every learner, evaluation suggests that involving creative practitioners in delivering the curriculum has myriad benefits.

- Many learners will be engaged by the novelty of a new face in the room, perhaps with a very different perspective on life than they have previously experienced at home or in school. This can extend their sphere of experience considerably and open new doors in terms of their own aspirations.

- Some learners will thrive on the different approaches to a learning experience taken by the creative practitioners. Learning can be supported in subject areas that were previously difficult and can help realise learner potential and boost confidence for future learning situations.

- Some learners come into their own when out of the school environment in a place that they see as belonging to the world to which they might one day aspire. This can result in a new maturity of approach and a willingness to participate in something they perceive as real.

- Teachers and trainees can learn from some of the approaches employed by creative practitioners and knit them into their own future practice.
- Practitioners gain in terms of self-awareness, confidence, idea generation and, of course, in terms of income that will often subsidise their personal creative endeavours.
- Overall, society benefits from a population of young people who are open-minded, confident in their creativity and comfortable in cultural venues and environments.

Ultimately, with the right stimulus, environment and objectives young people will become problem solvers, team players, analysts, evaluators and critical thinkers, and all the time many will probably forget they are even learning until it comes to reflecting on their experiences. When they look back in later life on their formal education many will remember those stand-out moments and the teachers involved in providing them.

Discussion points

- How could a relationship with a local arts organisation enhance the delivery of your curriculum in terms of learner experience?
- With limited resources, why should schools still consider prioritising learning outside the classroom?
- What gaps in your current skills base could you fill through a co-delivery experience with a creative practitioner?

References

Bluecoat (no date) *About Bluecoat*. Available online at www.thebluecoat.org.uk (accessed 18 July 2012).

National Advisory Committee on Creative and Cultural Education (NACCCE) (1999) *All Our Futures: Creativity, culture and education* (The Robinson Report), London: HMSO.

7

Barriers, enablers and practical approaches

Steve Padget

Key questions

- What are the current barriers to and enablers of creative learning and teaching?

- What methodologies exist to help teachers develop a classroom in which the environment is conducive to creative learning and teaching?

- How can creative learning be harnessed as a force for change?

The writers of this book, looking at creativity and critical thinking from a variety of viewpoints, have described a range of successful innovations and practices. We have seen how the creativity, vision and the intrinsic motivation of the teacher are powerful factors in this, but also that support must come from the ethos of the school if these ventures are to be successful. We have seen how wide the benefits can be to learners when creative methodologies are adopted by teachers who understand their power. It is hoped that teachers, in practice and in training, on reading these chapters will be inspired to see how they can become part of a movement that is based on a child-centred, sociocultural view of learning.

Barriers and enablers

Embedded within our current education practices at school level and wider are factors that act as enablers of creativity and those that act as barriers. Consequently there are tensions and dilemmas that schools have to resolve if they are to be part of the movement towards the greater inclusion of creativity in the education that they provide.

The three principal barriers are: the use of competition as a driver of improvement, the attempted standardisation of learning and teaching through the National Curriculum and its associated strategies, and the use of stringent testing and assessment against externally imposed criteria (Sahlberg 2010a). The effect of these measures has been shown to narrow the curriculum and the pedagogic choices available to teachers, to emphasise the worth of individual achievement above collaborative endeavour, and to generate a climate of reform, the rationale for which has been to provide schools with an edge to compete for finite resources rather than improve the learning (Sahlberg 2010a).

Enablers of creativity have been seen to be: collaboration within and between schools, the development of cooperative learning in classrooms with the associated risk taking, and a culture of learning how to handle the possibility of being wrong (Sahlberg 2010a). The benefits of collaboration and cooperation are many and to be seen at all levels and across all aspects of the work of the institution. The resultant environment of mutual respect allows for innovation involving risk taking, something that cannot happen without the presence of confidence and trust. For an institution to show that it values the sometimes uncertain process of creativity it has to reward good ideas and innovative solutions and not only the achievement of right answers.

Sahlberg discusses the paradox that exists in European education – that in order for the nations of Europe to compete more effectively on the knowledge-based global stage our schools, teachers and learners need to compete less. He suggests that at all levels of the educational process more effectiveness would be achieved by the development of a greater level of cooperation and networking. 'Co-operation and networking rather than competition and disconnectedness should therefore lead the education policies and development of education systems' (Sahlberg 2010b). That much practice throughout education in the UK seems currently frozen into the ground is a result of policies demanding uniformity of outcome, the use of a 'state theory of learning' (Watkins 2010) and compliance with external standards. The resultant individualisation of teachers' work, the commoditisation of education and the setting of school against school has done little to enhance the desire of institutions to cooperate.

Recent research in the UK has found a wide variation in the approaches of teachers to issues of creativity across the phases. The pattern of evidence found suggests that, while creativity thrives in the lower key stages by the time KS3 and 4 are reached, the pressure to conform to the assessment demands of the National Curriculum has narrowed the task opportunities offered. Teachers were seen to abandon those tasks that involved exploration and collaboration, preferring to focus increasingly on those tasks that valued individual performance. It is suggested that this change of stance reflects the pressure of external assessment that becomes increasingly acute in the later stages (Craft and Cremin *et al.* 2007).

Despite the implications of these findings there is a growing body of methodology rooted in the principles of creative, collaborative and cooperative learning to which schools are subscribing in varied measures. The report *All Our Futures* (NACCCE 1999) recognises the crucial role of education leaders in this and recommends that they should be supported in the establishment of an 'organisational climate and framework for creativity'. This is a recognition of the place of creativity as part of the ethos of a school and that creativity is something that should pervade all aspects of the work; this is the small 'c' creativity that needs to infuse planning and teaching practices.

The Ofsted report of 2010, *Learning: Creative approaches that raise standards*, although rather hemmed in by the PLTS agenda, shows that across the 44 schools visited there was a great deal of creativity woven into the fabric of the curriculum enhancing, says the report, rather than replacing the provision of the National Curriculum. The report says that 'In schools with good teaching, there is not a conflict between the National Curriculum, national standards in core subjects and creative approaches to learning' (p. 5), and further:

> Teachers were seen to promote creative learning most purposefully and effectively when encouraging pupils to question and challenge, make connections and see relationships, speculate, keep options open while pursuing a line of enquiry, and reflect critically on ideas, actions and results.
>
> (pp. 5–6)

The report saw, unsurprisingly, that the following combination of factors when present in a school would provide the foundation for successful creative learning:

- well-organised cross-curricular links that allowed scope for independent enquiry;
- inclusiveness, ensuring that it was accessible and relevant to all pupils;
- a focus on experiential learning, with knowledge, understanding and skills developed through first-hand, practical experience and evaluation;
- well-integrated use of technology;
- effective preparation of pupils for the next stage of their learning, training or employment;
- a broad and accessible enrichment programme;
- clear and well-supported links with the local community and cultures, often drawing on local knowledge and experience to enhance pupils' learning;
- a flexible approach to timetabling to accommodate extended, whole-school or whole-year activities;

- partnerships that extended pupils' opportunities for creative learning.

(Ofsted 2010: 8)

Elsewhere in this book, the writers look at the practical side of creative learning. There are examples of practice that amplify the importance of some of the points above, namely: the benefits that come from timetable flexibility (Chapter 5), enabling groups of learners to experience a different intensity of learning experience; the value to learners of projects developing Creative Partnerships (Chapters 4 and 6), where external agencies can be used to inject the excitement that comes from doing things in a different way; and the benefits of 'clear and well-supported links with the local community and cultures' (also Chapter 4), where the active involvement of parents and families in whole-school and whole-year learning enriches the experience. Creativity is seen in the breadth, variety and value of such initiatives as schools endeavour to generate a 'climate and framework for creativity'.

The 'climate and framework for creativity' can be seen in the public statements of schools that have embraced the idea of becoming one of the 55 Thinking Schools in the UK or one of the 50 or so Schools of Creativity. Below are some examples of mission statements from these schools, which show their ability to look at teaching and learning in an altogether more holistic way:

We aim to provide an environment in which your child feels stimulated and in which he/she will learn to become a more independent creative thinker with a lively and enquiring mind.

(An example from a primary school)

Learning may be defined as 'a process of undergoing personal change' and as such the school recognises that it is what the learner thinks, says and does that creates the learning not what the teacher thinks, says and does.

(An example from a secondary school)

Creativity as a motivator of learning

The statements of intent above include the creation of an appropriate environment, recognition of the value of a learner-centred stance and an acknowledgement of the position of creativity in learning processes. The creation of the right environment with its physical, emotional and intellectual components is seen by many as being key to the development of intrinsic motivation in learners and teachers alike. Amabile (1998) looks at the factors that enhance intrinsic motivation and sees the value of an environment that contains the right level of challenge, freedom to choose how to solve a problem, and having the right time and tools, these being underpinned by encouragement and support from both outside and within well-structured working groups.

Motivation was also investigated by Dweck (1986) and across a range of learners striking differences were observed in the cognitive performance of those who were motivated by performance goals when compared with those whose motivation was in terms of learning goals. The strong orientation of the learners motivated by performance goals was towards the avoidance of risk and challenge, which contrasted markedly with the more positive, enquiring attitudes of those motivated by learning goals. Those with learning–goal motivation were much more effective in harnessing their abilities in the pursuit of the solutions to problems and they more readily initiated and engaged with activities that would promote intellectual growth, gaining more satisfaction from the process. The creation of a classroom ethos that encourages learning goals is therefore of great importance and this is what we see when we look at the range of methodologies that have been developed for use in schools.

Methodologies

It is useful at this point to look at the increasing number of very accessible and effective classroom techniques in terms of four broad and overlapping areas:

- the strengthening of learning dispositions;
- the development of a community of enquiry;
- the use of thinking tools;
- methods of cognitive acceleration.

The importance of disposition

Building Learning Power (BLP), devised by Guy Claxton and colleagues from the University of Bristol, challenges teachers and learners to look at learning in terms of the dispositions of Resilience, Resourcefulness, Reflectiveness and Reciprocity and how these can be actively developed to enhance learning (see also Chapters 1 and 5). Each of these dispositions is made up of a series of learning behaviours, 'capacities' as they are called by the authors, and the underlying belief is that each of these can be developed by learners given the right opportunity. This is a school-wide strategic approach that impacts not only on what happens in the classroom, but also on what the whole school says about learning and the vision for the preparation of learners for an uncertain future (Claxton *et al.* 2011: 2).

'A central concern of Building Learning Power is with enabling students to become more self aware as learners, to develop the habits of a successful learner, and to appreciate that they can continually improve those habits' (Gornall *et al.* 2005: 5). This work was built on and developed in the ELLI (Effective Lifelong Learning Index) project. Both BLP and ELLI emphasise the need to create a language that can be used to articulate the importance of learning itself, which learners and teachers can share in order to be successful. The authors of the ELLI project echo Harrington's (1990) notion of the creative ecosystem when they talk about the ecology of learning and the need to balance the broad elements of value, attitude and disposition in the classroom in order to promote the development of the whole person. (Deakin Crick 2006: 2–3).

An example of a similar approach is 'Habits of Mind' (HoM) devised by Art Costa and Bena Kallick (n.d.), who say: 'A "Habit of Mind" means having a disposition toward behaving intelligently when confronted with problems, the answers to which are not immediately known.' The proponents of HoM stress the importance of using pedagogic approaches that strike a balance between learners' achievement of the necessary cognitive skills and their acquisition of life skills such as persistence, risk taking and metacognition.

Over the last ten years the Royal Society of Arts' Opening Minds curriculum has attracted over two hundred schools in the UK to a vision of a competence-based model of learning and teaching. By focusing the learning around the five 'key competences' of Citizenship, Learning, Managing Information, Relating to People and Managing Situations (CLIPS), they aim to be 'reclaiming ownership of learning' and making a coherent whole of the National Curriculum, which they say is composed of a jigsaw of fragments that don't really fit together. These five competences and their component subsections provide an unarguable and comprehensive list of the skills and attributes that are needed by learners who are going to be making their way in the twenty-first-century world. The vision is of a school-wide learning strategy expressly geared to providing a curriculum that promotes the development of the five competences above, thus providing a solid foundation of skills that will be needed in KS4 and beyond. This model is seen to promote improved motivation and a confident approach to independent learning.

Creating a community of enquiry

Philosophy for Children (P4C) and Mantle of the Expert (MoE) are approaches built on the idea of creating a community of enquiry. Devised by Matthew Lipman, P4C 'aims to encourage children and adults to think critically, caringly, creatively and collaboratively'. This method builds a 'community of enquiry' where participants create and enquire into their own questions, and 'learn how to learn' in the process (Sapere 2010). Learners move, in a spirit of enquiry, beyond information to seek understanding and thus transform reflection. If enquiry is placed centre stage the classroom becomes the community of enquiry. Friendship and cooperation are welcomed as positive contributions to the learning atmosphere and replace the 'semi-adversarial and competitive conditions' that frequently exist (Lipman 2003: 94). When these conditions are achieved the aim of P4C is realised: to improve the critical, the creative and the caring thinking of learners.

Rather than lessons, the proponents of P4C prefer to talk about 'enquiries', which follow a set procedure allowing the community of enquiry to be formed and to operate effectively. The use of the word 'enquiry' is important – it takes the focus from the teacher and the dispensing of knowledge and places it with the words and thoughts of the participants and the cooperative processes of making meaning and understanding. The merits of questions generated by the learners in response to a chosen stimulus are discussed before the key question is democratically decided upon. The process of deciding which question to address is an important part of the enquiry as it encourages active participation and allows learners to understand how decisions can be made and how to listen to and take into account other points of view.

Mantle of the Expert (MoE) was developed by Dorothy Heathcote and is 'a drama-inquiry approach to teaching and learning' (Mantle of the Expert n.d.). Another technique using the community of enquiry principle, MoE can be powerful in many areas of the curriculum. Groups of learners take on the role of experts – explorers, archaeologists, escaping refugees – as they find solutions to problems and answers to questions. Learners are able to take ownership of what is called the 'enterprise' as they take on 'the mantle of the expert' and benefit from being able to see issues through the eyes of others.

Thinking tools

The third type of methodology, which is very wide in scope, consists of a range of powerful techniques usually called thinking tools. Starting from the premise that creative thinking is a complex of skills that must be actively developed, these widely available tactical classroom techniques involve the use of specific props and procedures to create problem-solving opportunities for groups of learners across the age and ability range. As with any set of tools, specific techniques have specific uses and the creative teacher will use the tool that is appropriate for a particular task, bearing in mind the needs and aptitudes of the learners.

Edward de Bono's Thinking Hats is one such technique (de Bono 2000) and is discussed at length in Chapter 4. Familiar to many are the liberating effects of this technique, which has migrated over the years from business training into schools, where it frequently takes its place in a teacher's repertoire of creative methodologies. Learners take on problems and discuss solutions using the different characteristics and viewpoints represented by each different-coloured hat. The key to the success of this method is the separation of the individual from the opinion, each hat representing a different way of looking at the issue in question, giving an empowering effect that allows learners to think for themselves as big problems are broken down into more manageable chunks. Associated with this is the CoRT (Cognitive Research Trust) material. The six sections of the CoRT Thinking Programme (CoRT for Schools) provide a detailed and structured approach to the explicit teaching of thinking skills, emphasising de Bono's assertion that learners' capacities for 'constructive thinking' in real life need to be increased.

TASC (Thinking Actively in a Social Context), a 'thinking-skills framework' devised by Belle Wallace, is an example of a methodology that looks at the process of developing learners' thinking in a collaborative eight-stage process (TASC 2010). It begins with gathering knowledge that learners already possess as they identify the problem and the questions that it poses. Ideas generated are selected, then implemented. The processes of evaluating, communicating the ideas to someone else and reflecting on the experience complete the cycle. The core feature of this method is the staged process – the breaking down of a problem into manageable chunks by using the interrelated stages of the process – which allows learners to move together from what they already know to the understanding of something new, which is shown by their ability to articulate the new learning to others.

There are parallels between this method and another technique that takes learners through a staged thinking process. In using the LogoVisual Thinking (LVT) tools small groups of learners move through a cyclical core process that begins with focusing on the problem, the task, expressed in an open 'key question'. Then, by gathering what is already known and putting responses to the key question in short sentences on repositionable shapes, thoughts can be arranged, grouped and rearranged as the discussion develops (Best *et al.* 2005). This technique has the ability to show new and sometimes unexpected and original relationships between thoughts and ideas as they are juxtaposed on the board in the organising phase of the process. This is followed by the final stage, that of the application of the new understandings in response to the original challenge. The process allows the development of learners' deeply valuable talk, which facilitates the decision-making process. The benefits of this method are several and include the following:

- The tactile and visual aspects of this tool are appreciated by many learners, as is the physical flexibility that allows changes of mind to be seen and discussed as the shapes are arranged and rearranged based on the new thinking that emerges actively from the discussion. The thoughts can be permanent or they can be temporary.

- Learners can understand the importance of their own contributions as they see their thoughts in relation to those of others; they begin to appreciate the democracy of the process, the synergy of the whole and their part in that process.

- The board provides the medium to integrate thinking, bringing together into new patterns the diverse thoughts of the members of the group.

- The use of large boards means that groups can easily show, discuss and share their ideas with others within and beyond the working group.

- The visibility of the board allows teachers and other learners to see not only what the group is thinking, but *how* the group is thinking.

LVT is a powerful tool that has the capacity to promote the development of the skills of information processing, reasoning, enquiry, creative thinking and critical thinking. Figure 7.1 shows an array of ideas that came from a recent examination of the effects of crime and criminality on young people. The cluster has been given a title to articulate the dynamic of that gathering of thoughts.

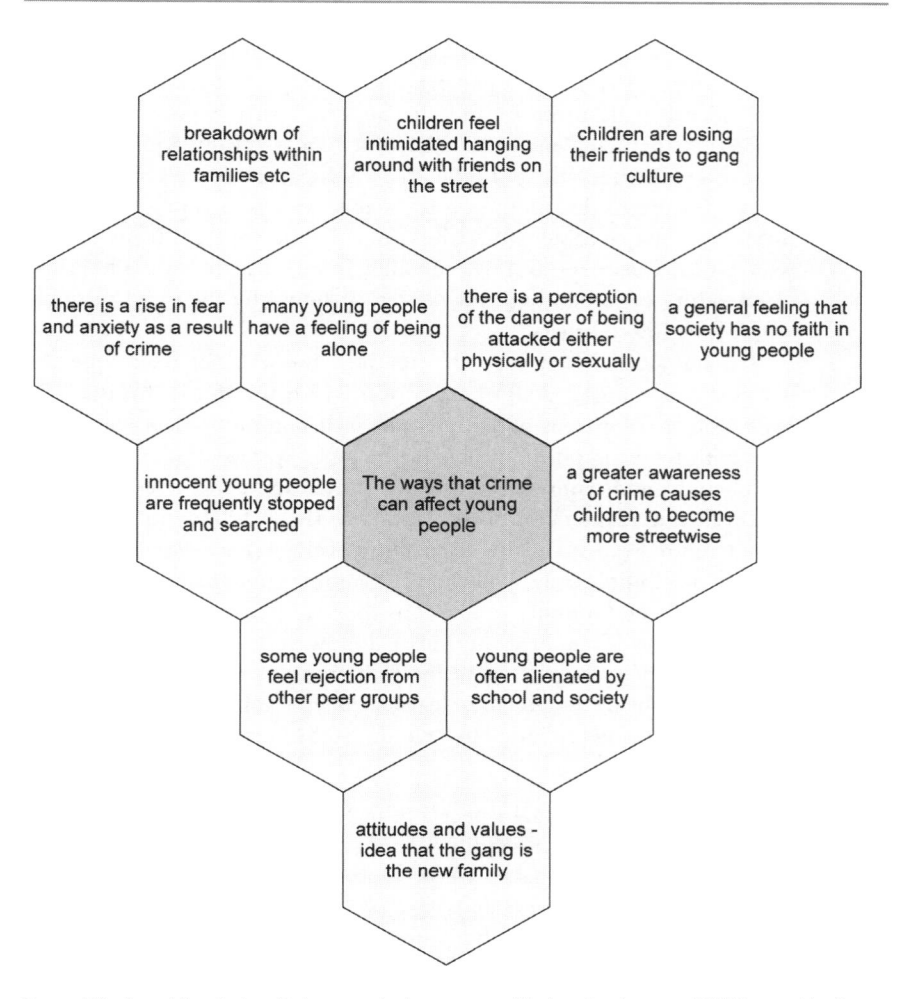

Figure 7.1 One of the clusters that emerged when a group of trainee teachers used LVT to consider the effects of crime on young people

Accelerating the learning

Mind mapping, devised by Tony Buzan (ThinkBuzan n.d.), is a technique that dates from the mid-1970s. It was the first of the 'brain-based learning' techniques that were informed by rapid developments in neuroscience and the understanding of how we learn. It continues to be a very influential and distinctively graphical technique used in schools to boost memory and accelerate learning. This technique enables learners to generate and organise ideas on paper the better to recall them and their relationships later. Mind mapping is beneficial for individual work but it is also effective when carried out by a group.

Philip Adey and Michael Shayer (1994), in their exploration of cognitive acceleration (Cognitive Acceleration through Science Education – CASE), sought to demonstrate a method of promoting learners' thinking from concrete to abstract by means of a specific lesson structure. This was done by building on the constructivist idea that learners need to create meaning for themselves and do this best in the context of a working group.

The lesson consists of five parts:

1   An introduction which sets the scene (concrete preparation).
2   A puzzle or challenge which needs to be solved (cognitive conflict).
3   Group-work and discussion where pupils share ideas for solutions (social construction).
4   Explaining the thinking which gave the answer (metacognition).
5   Making links to everyday applications of the ideas discussed (bridging).

(Adey and Shayer 1994: 78)

One of the key findings of this work was that the effect on the learners was that their performance improved not only in the science lessons, but also in English and maths, thus demonstrating the successful improvement of generic learning skills.

Methods based on an understanding of Howard Gardner's multiple intelligences theory (1983) and the findings of cognitive science are also seen as accelerating learning. The term 'Accelerated Learning' was coined in 1985 by Colin Rose in his book of that title, where he articulated the principles, values and advantages that underpin what was called 'brain-based learning'. Further exploration of Accelerated Learning followed with Alistair Smith's *Accelerated Learning in Practice* (1998) and Oliver Caviglioli and Ian Harris's *Mapwise* (2000). These approaches have been influential in the way that learning is managed in many schools and, in each approach, the understanding is that critical-thinking processes are intertwined with factual knowledge, that 'factual knowledge must precede skill' (Willingham 2009: 30), underlining the importance of infusing the two in the design and delivery of learning.

The emphasis in Accelerated Learning techniques is on the physical readiness of the learners, their psychological readiness and the use of teaching techniques that will appeal to all preferred learning styles in the context of a highly structured four-part sequence of challenging and engaging learning activities (Smith 1998). Between these 10–15-minute lesson chunks are breaks of 1–2 minutes, designed to allow learners to process what has just been taught. This structure, with the use of selected music as a background, is designed to be conducive to learning and deliver the optimum learning conditions.

A compendium of creative learning and teaching methodologies with references to books, guidance and links to websites can be found in Appendix 1.

Learning as a constructive, social process

As we look at the each of these creative approaches two common factors emerge. First, we see that there is the understanding that learning is a constructive and essentially social process; second, in the design and delivery of the learning the cognitive and the curricular objectives should be infused.

Success in the first of these depends on the deliberate creation of an environment in which learner collaboration is encouraged; this is a necessary precursor to the successful use of cooperative learning strategies. (Chapter 5 shows how this can work practically in the context of Year 8 geography and outlines the planning, resourcing and operational implications.) When suitable conditions are created learners are able to work together to maximise their own learning and that of others and, in consequence, interpersonal skills develop alongside cognitive skills. It has been shown (Johnson and Johnson 1990) that both collaborative and cooperative learning arrangements are highly effective in the promotion of thinking if a range of elements exist:

- clearly perceived positive interdependence;
- face-to face-interaction;
- individual accountability;
- the teaching of collaborative skills;
- group processing.

Cooperative learning is dynamic and highly organised. When it is effective it is often characterised by the use of role play, and it will have cognitive, metacognitive and social learning objectives and, significantly, a communication structure characterised by learners engaging 'in extensive verbal negotiations with peers' (Jacobs *et al.* 1997). Cooperative approaches such as Kagan Cooperative Learning (Kagan and Kagan 2009) emphasise continually the need to build up and maintain team spirit among group members and a high level of interconnectedness and awareness of the processes in which they are participating. The Jigsaw Cooperative Learning (2011) method similarly emphasises positive interdependence and individual accountability, considered essential if a thinking environment is to be created. In this, as with other cooperative methods, Jigsaw learners need to be connected to the learning, communicating with each other, and have an awareness of their roles and responsibilities within the group.

The second common factor is the infusion of cognitive objectives and learning objectives (see Chapter 1). That is to say, the learning processes are made explicit as learners are helped to discover how the engine works as well as where they are on the map, where their destination is and what route they need to take. The work done by Ennis (1997), McGuinness (2000), Marin and Halpern (2010) and others has led to the conclusion that, for learners of all ages and abilities, leaving the development of social learning and interpersonal skills to chance is not an option; the necessary learning skills and their value have to be discussed as much as content issues. These are the lifelong learning skills, the dispositions, the habits of mind, the creativity that underpins an individual's ability to be successful.

Endpiece

The foregoing chapters have cast light on elements of the theoretical base of creativity and critical thinking and explored some of the possibilities that exist for the practical application of these concepts across a wide range of learning settings, from community-conscious work in a KS2 setting, through the secondary phases and on into teacher training. The factor that binds these chapters is the potential for enrichment seen in the practices described as a greater understanding of creative learning, creative thinking and critical thinking is achieved. These are complex concepts and teachers who appreciate their power and value are showing a fundamental and deep commitment to breaking the mould – to challenging the status quo, but above all they are showing their own creativity in their transactions in the classroom.

It is my belief that creativity and critical thinking should be seen in three ways:

- as closely related dynamic concepts;
- as being integral to our understanding of learning and teaching; and
- as being powerful drivers for change and improvements in teaching.

Closely related dynamic concepts

Creativity and critical thinking have deep psychological, sociological and philosophical roots and an examination of these concepts can cause us to ask some searching questions about what teachers are and what teachers do. We see that they are related – they have a symbiotic relationship and to foster one is to promote the other. Further, we can see how the function and practice of teachers will be conditioned by the broader cultural context because neither creativity nor critical thinking is culture-neutral and educational practices and policies inevitably reflect the values and aspirations of the culture in which they are situated.

Integral to the processes of learning

We have seen that, by thinking about creativity in the context of learning, we focus on the very processes of learning itself and, in so doing, we examine what learners are actually doing in our classes and for what purpose. We note the empowerment to learn that comes from the use of collaborative and cooperative learning methodologies; we note also the importance of language, that most significant cultural tool, not thinking of it just as the medium of learning, but as part of the learning mechanism itself. Given this understanding we need to reappraise the value and function of the language life of the classroom – the interchanges between teachers and learners and those between the learners themselves – and understand what these say about their relative positions in a sociocultural view of learning. These factors profoundly influence the planning, the delivery and the organisation of learning. The writers of this book have all taken a fresh look at learning and teaching, and the propagation of a language-friendly learning environment has been an essential first step, seen as a prerequisite for the success of the learning because it is part of the process of learning.

The work described in Chapter 5 showed two important visible benefits. There was the benefit to the learners gained by being able to work socially in a language-rich learning environment and there was the benefit to the young teachers – they were able to see how their role changed and how the language dynamic changed. Having planned these episodes for learners with whom they were familiar, the teachers were also able to see how much more responsive both the groups were than when constrained by the normal lesson arrangements.

Drivers for change in teaching

In teaching creatively the attitudes and activities of classroom professionals demonstrate the acceptance of a set of values, articulated in Chapter 1, which define the way their work is carried out and define the nature of the work space they inhabit. In creative teaching lies the seed of creative learning based on the idea of looking for possibilities in the co-constructed, co-owned joint endeavour. When teachers use their creativity an environment is generated where learners can 'maintain and develop their own creative learning' (Craft 2005). This suggests a dynamic situation the detail of which will change from phase to phase, but the principles hold good for all, as does the practitioner's need to know that their approaches are supported by colleagues and contribute to the shared ethos of the school.

In Chapter 4 we saw the impact of thinking about learning and teaching in a creative way in the scope and vision of the 'Keeping Warm' and 'Bad Word' projects. By looking beyond the school gates and into the community the depth and value of the work was enhanced, the whole school became involved and cooperative working became the norm – all of the school community gained lasting benefit from this work. Some of this has been in terms of lasting changes in the shared view of learning and teaching manifested in the development of methodologies incorporating the ideas that came from taking part in the Creative Partnerships projects.

That change is necessary in the management of education is clear and the current model of learning and teaching in many ways is not fit for purpose. In Claxton's words, we need to make our schools more like learning gymnasia rather than the old assembly line and monastery models that are still frequently to be found (Claxton 2008). They need to be places 'where children go to have their "learning stamina" developed and their "learning muscles" stretched' (Claxton 2008: 127). And this, he says, not simply to pass exams 'but so they can be confident, capable, powerful learners for the rest of their lives' (Claxton 2008: 127). The micro-management of the processes of learning produces institutions that compete with one another, some more effectively than others; it does not encourage the development of those personal skills that learners need if they are to be well-informed and well-motivated citizens. Ian Gilbert (2011), in his introduction to *Why Do I Need a Teacher When I've Got Google?*, states that there are many good teachers who are not doing a *bad* job, but doing the *wrong* job – and that traditional teaching may be antithetical to the needs of twenty-first-century learning.

The continued development of structures within schools that promote and support independent thinking and learning is essential. Schools that use such phrases as 'shaping the future through creative learning' in their literature are those that have taken a long look at the processes of learning and teaching and have seen not only the need for change but how that change can be brought about. Those schools that refer to their charges as 'learning partners' have examined the change in the teacher–learner relationship that develops when the implications of creative learning and teaching are put into practice. These are the institutions that have realised that nineteenth-century methods are not those that will adequately prepare learners for life in the twenty-first century and, despite the very real pressure to conform, these schools are overcoming the barriers to creative learning and some, supported by such organisations as the RSA (the Royal Society for the encouragement of Arts, Manufactures and Commerce), are adopting competence-based approaches capable of addressing a different way of looking at learning. There are Schools of Creativity where homework becomes an Independent Learning programme, an integral part of a KS3 curriculum that also includes problem-based learning tasks with the stated intention of promoting independent learning and developing problem-solving and communication skills across the curriculum.

In schools such as these the need to value and facilitate the development of the processes of learning as well as the products is recognised, as is the need to develop learning and teaching models that promote in learners the ability to reflect and develop a sense of self. In schools such as these the reforms that have taken place over time are systemic, not cosmetic, and are to do with how effective the schools can be in achieving their primary pursuit. Returning to Aronowitz, we remind ourselves that 'the active knower, not the mind as a repository of "information", is the goal of education' (1998: 14).

Discussion points

- How can school managers develop a school's ethos based on the principles of creative learning and teaching to better educate the citizens of the twenty-first century?

- How can curriculum managers support departmental teams in their understanding, competence and confidence in using a range of creative teaching methodologies?

- How can class teachers be supported in their creation of a learning environment in the classroom where the power of creative learning is evident?

Useful websites/resources

www.campaignforlearning.org.uk   The Campaign for Learning.
www.creative-partnerships.com/about/schools-of-crea-
   tivity   Creative Partnerships' Schools of Creativity programme.
www.debonofoundation.co.uk   The de Bono Foundation.
www.enquiringminds.org.uk   Futurelab's *Enquiring Minds* website.
www.hvlc.org.uk/ace/aifl/docs/highlandmodel/toolsforthinking.
   pdf   Fisher's *Tools for Thinking* can be found here.
www.openingminds.org.uk   The RSA's *Opening Minds* website.
www.sapere.org.uk   The home of Philosophy for Children.
www.teachernet.org.uk   Teachernet.
www.woodnewton.northants.sch.uk   Woodnewton Primary School,
   Corby, Northants – an example of a learning community as a
   Thinking School.
Best, B. and Thomas, W. (2008) *The Creative Teaching and Learning
   Resource Book*, London and New York: Continuum.
Gilbert, I. (2011) *Why Do I Need a Teacher When I've Got Google?*,
   London and New York: Routledge.
Gornall, S., Chambers, M. and Claxton, G. (2005) *Building Learning
   Power in Action*, Bristol: TLO.
Willingham, D.T. (2009) *Why Students Don't Like School*, San Francisco,
   CA: Jossey-Bass.

References

Adey, P. and Shayer, M. (1994) *Really Raising Standards: Cognitive intervention and academic achievement*, London: Routledge.
Amabile, T. (1998) 'How to kill creativity', *Harvard Business Review*, Sept.–Oct. 1998.
Aronowitz, S. (1998) 'Introduction', in Freire, P., *Pedagogy of Freedom* (translated from Portuguese by P. Clarke), Oxford: Rowman and Littlefield.
Best, B., Blake, A. and Varney, J. (2005) *Making Meaning: Learning through LogoVisual Thinking*, Cambridge: Chris Kington.
Caviglioli, O. and Harris, I. (2000) *Mapwise: Accelerated Learning through visual thinking*, London: Continuum.
Claxton, G. (2008) *What's the Point of School?*, Oxford: One World Publications.
Claxton, G., Chambers, M., Powell, G. and Lucas, B. (2011) *The Learning Powered School*, Bristol: TLO.
Costa, A.L. and Kallick, B. (no date) *Habits of Mind*. Available online at www.institute-forhabitsofmind.com (accessed 22 September 2011).

Craft, A. (2005) *Creativity in Schools: Tensions and dilemmas*, Oxford: Routledge.

Craft, A., Cremin, T., Burnard, P. and Chappell, K. (2007) 'Teacher stance in creative learning: a study of progression', *Journal of Thinking Skills and Creativity*, 2(2): 136–47.

Deakin Crick, R. (2006) *Learning Power in Action*, London: Paul Chapman Publishing.

de Bono, E. (2000) *Six Thinking Hats*, London: Penguin.

Dweck, C. (1986) 'Motivational processes affecting learning', *American Psychologist*, 41(10): 1040–8.

Ennis, R.H. (1997) 'Incorporating thinking skills into the curriculum: an introduction to some basic issues', *Inquiry: Critical Thinking Across the Disciplines*, 16(3): 1–9.

Gardner, H. (1983) *Frames of Mind: The theory of multiple intelligences*, New York: Basic Books.

Gilbert, I. (2011) *Why Do I Need a Teacher When I've Got Google?*, London and New York: Routledge.

Gornall, S., Chambers, M. and Claxton, G. (2005) *Building Learning Power in Action*, Bristol: TLO.

Harrington, D.M. (1990) 'The ecology of human creativity: a psychological perspective', in Runco, M.A. and Albert, R.S. (eds) *Theories of Creativity*, London: Sage.

Jacobs, G.M., Lee, C. and Ng, M. (1997) 'Co-operative learning in the thinking classroom', paper presented at the International Conference on Thinking, Singapore.

Jigsaw Cooperative Learning (2011) *Jigsaw Classroom*. Available online at www.jigsaw.org (accessed 28 November 2011).

Johnson, D.W. and Johnson, R.T. (1990) 'Cooperative learning and achievement', in Sharan, S. (ed.) *Cooperative Learning: Theory and research*, New York: Praeger, pp. 23–37.

Kagan, S. and Kagan, M. (2009) *Kagan Cooperative Learning*, San Clemente, CA: Kagan Publishing.

Lipman, M. (2003) *Thinking in Education* (2nd edn), New York: Cambridge University Press.

McGuinness, C. (2000) 'ACTS: a methodology for teaching thinking across the curriculum', *Teaching Thinking*, 2: 1–12.

Mantle of the Expert (no date) *What is MoE?* Available online at www.mantleoftheexpert.com (accessed 28 November 2011).

Marin, L.M. and Halpern, D.F. (2010) 'Pedagogy for developing critical thinking in adolescents: explicit instruction produces greatest gains', *Thinking Skills and Creativity*: Doi: 10.1016/j.tsc.2010.08.002.

National Advisory Committee on Creative and Cultural Education (NACCCE) (1999) *All Our Futures: Creativity, culture and education* (The Robinson Report), London: HMSO.

Ofsted (2010) *Learning: Creative approaches that raise standards*, Manchester: Ofsted.

Rose, C. (1985) *Accelerated Learning*, Aylesbury: Accelerated Learning Systems.

Sahlberg, P. (2010a) 'The role of education in promoting creativity: potential barriers and enabling factors', in Villalba, E. (ed.) *Measuring Creativity*, Luxemburg: OPOCE.

Sahlberg, P. (2010b) 'Global educational reform movement and national educational change', paper presented at the 2010 EUNEC Conference, Brussels, 2 December.

Sapere (2010) *Philosophy for Children*. Available online at www.sapere.org.uk (accessed 22 September 2011).

Smith, A. (1998) *Accelerated Learning in Practice*, Stafford: Network Educational Press.

Thinking Actively in a Social Context (TASC) (2010) *TASC Wheel*. Available online at www.tascwheel.com (accessed 22 September 2011).

Watkins, C. (2010) 'Learning, performance and improvement', *INSI Research Matters*, 34(Summer).

Willingham, D.T. (2009) *Why Students Don't Like School*, San Francisco, CA: Jossey-Bass.

Appendix 1

Creative learning and teaching

Key references and sources

Competence-based curriculum	Opening Minds	Developed by the RSA, www.rsaopeningminds.org.uk/about-rsa-openingminds/
Disposition	Habits of Mind	Art Costa and Bena Kallick, www.habitsofmind.co.uk/
	Building Learning Power	S. Gornall, M. Chambers and G. Claxton, *Building Learning Power in Action*, TLO, Bristol, 2005 G. Claxton, M. Chambers, G. Powell and B. Lucas, *The Learning Powered School*, TLO, Bristol, 2011
	Learning Power in Practice – the ELLI project	R. Deakin Crick, *Learning Power in Practice*, Paul Chapman, London, 2006
Community of Enquiry	Philosophy for Children (P4C)	Matthew Lipman, *Thinking in Education*, Cambridge University Press, 2003 (2nd edn, 2007) Sapere: http://sapere.org.uk/ Robert Fisher, *Teaching Thinking: Philosophical enquiry in the classroom* (3rd edn), Continuum, London, 2008

Community of Enquiry	Mantle of the Expert (MOE)	Dorothy Heathcote, Brian Edmiston and others, www.mantleoftheexpert.com/
	Thinking Through School	A. De A'Echevarria and D. Leat, *Thinking Through School* suite of books, 2006, www.teachingexpertise.com/articles/thinking-through-school-building-a-learning-community-1818
Thinking Tools	LogoVisual Thinking	Anthony Blake and John Varney, http://www.logovisual.com/ B. Best, A. Blake and J. Varney, *Making Meaning: Learning through LogoVisual Thinking*, Chris Kington, Cambridge, 2005
	The TASC Wheel (Thinking Actively in Social Contexts	Belle Wallace, www.tascwheel.com/
	Thinking Hats	Edward de Bono Foundation, http://debonoforschools.com/asp/six_hats.asp
	Cognitive Research Trust (CoRT1–6)	Edward de Bono Foundation, www.debonofoundation.co.uk/whycort.html
	Thinking Maps	David Hyerle and Chris Yeager, www.thinkingmaps.com/
	Mind Maps	Tony Buzan, www.thinkbuzan.com/uk/ and many readily available books
Accelerated Learning	Accelerated Learning and ALPS	Alistair Smith, www.acceleratedlearning.com/method/index.html
	Cognitive Acceleration in Science Education (CASE)	Philip Adey and Michael Shayer, *Really Raising Standards: Cognitive intervention and academic achievement*, Psychology Press, Hove, 1994
	Mapwise	Oliver Caviglioli and Ian Harris, *Accelerated Learning Through Visible Thinking*, Continuum, London, 2000
Other sources	Jigsaw Cooperative Classroom	Elliot Aronson, www.jigsaw.org/
	Kagan Structures – Cooperative Learning	www.kaganonline.com/index.php
	The Thinking Classroom	Mike Fleetham, www.thinkingclassroom.co.uk/
	Socratic Dialogue	Various sources, www.criticalthinking.org/pages/the-role-of-socratic-questioning-in-thinking-teaching-amp-learning/522

Appendix 2

Evidencing creativity in teaching

A guide for trainees

This shows where creativity and critical thinking will be most relevant as part of the assessment of achievement against the *Teachers' Standards* (Department for Education, 2012). Those standards are in italics where creativity and critical thinking can be part of the evidence of achievement.

A teacher must:

1 Set high expectations which inspire, motivate and challenge pupils

- *establish a safe and stimulating environment for pupils, rooted in mutual respect*
- set goals that stretch and challenge pupils of all backgrounds, abilities and dispositions
- demonstrate consistently the positive attitudes, values and behaviour which are expected of pupils.

2 Promote good progress and outcomes by pupils

- be accountable for pupils' attainment, progress and outcomes
- *be aware of pupils' capabilities and their prior knowledge, and plan teaching to build on these*
- *guide pupils to reflect on the progress they have made and their emerging needs*

- *demonstrate knowledge and understanding of how pupils learn and how this impacts on teaching*
- encourage pupils to take a responsible and conscientious attitude to their own work and study.

3 Demonstrate good subject and curriculum knowledge

- *have a secure knowledge of the relevant subject(s) and curriculum areas, foster and maintain pupils' interest in the subject, and address misunderstandings*
- demonstrate a critical understanding of developments in the subject and curriculum areas, and promote the value of scholarship
- *demonstrate an understanding of and take responsibility for promoting high standards of literacy, articulacy and the correct use of standard English, whatever the teacher's specialist subject*
- if teaching early reading, demonstrate a clear understanding of systematic synthetic phonics
- if teaching early mathematics, demonstrate a clear understanding of appropriate teaching strategies.

4 Plan and teach well-structured lessons

- *impart knowledge and develop understanding through effective use of lesson time*
- *promote a love of learning and children's intellectual curiosity*
- set homework and plan other out-of-class activities to consolidate and extend the knowledge and understanding pupils have acquired
- reflect systematically on the effectiveness of lessons and approaches to teaching
- *contribute to the design and provision of an engaging curriculum within the relevant subject area(s).*

5 Adapt teaching to respond to the strengths and needs of all pupils

- *know when and how to differentiate appropriately, using approaches which enable pupils to be taught effectively*
- have a secure understanding of how a range of factors can inhibit pupils' ability to learn, and how best to overcome these
- demonstrate an awareness of the physical, social and intellectual development of children, and know how to adapt teaching to support pupils' education at different stages of development
- *have a clear understanding of the needs of all pupils, including those with special educational needs; those of high ability; those with English as an additional language; those with disabilities; and be able to use and evaluate distinctive teaching approaches to engage and support them.*

6 Make accurate and productive use of assessment

- know and understand how to assess the relevant subject and curriculum areas, including statutory assessment requirements
- make use of formative and summative assessment to secure pupils' progress
- use relevant data to monitor progress, set targets, and plan subsequent lessons
- give pupils regular feedback, both orally and through accurate marking, and encourage pupils to respond to the feedback.

7 Manage behaviour effectively to ensure a good and safe learning environment

- have clear rules and routines for behaviour in classrooms, and take responsibility for promoting good and courteous behaviour both in classrooms and around the school, in accordance with the school's behaviour policy
- have high expectations of behaviour, and establish a framework for discipline with a range of strategies, using praise, sanctions and rewards consistently and fairly
- *manage classes effectively, using approaches which are appropriate to pupils' needs in order to involve and motivate them*
- maintain good relationships with pupils, exercise appropriate authority, and act decisively when necessary.

8 Fulfil wider professional responsibilities

- make a positive contribution to the wider life and ethos of the school
- develop effective professional relationships with colleagues, knowing how and when to draw on advice and specialist support
- deploy support staff effectively
- take responsibility for improving teaching through appropriate professional development, responding to advice and feedback from colleagues
- communicate effectively with parents with regard to pupils' achievements and well-being.

(Source: www.education.gov.uk/publications/eOrderingDownload/ teachers%20standards.pdf)

Index